So, you ~~want to be a~~

RACING
DRIVER?

www.veloce.co.uk

First published in November 2021 by Veloce Publishing Limited, Veloce House, Parkway Farm Business Park, Middle Farm Way, Poundbury, Dorchester DT1 3AR, England. Tel +44 (0)1305 260068 / Fax 01305 250479 / e-mail info@veloce.co.uk / web www.veloce.co.uk or www.velocebooks.com. ISBN: 978-1-787117-43-3; UPC: 6-36847-01743-9.

So, you want to be a

RACING DRIVER?

Everything you need to know to start motor racing in karts and cars in the UK

BY
LEANNE FAHY

VELOCE PUBLISHING
THE PUBLISHER OF FINE AUTOMOTIVE BOOKS

CONTENTS

FOREWORD

I have been around the motorsport world for many years now, and raced at all levels, from karting through to international motorsport. I am currently racing for Jaguar in the FIA Formula E Championship, as well as with Ferrari in the FIA World Endurance Championship. I'm honoured to be asked to write this Foreword for Leanne, and I only wish this book had been available to me in my early days, as it would have helped a great deal:

I was just five when I started to get the motor racing bug, in 1992, and nagged my parents to let me start karting. It wasn't possible to start until I was eight, so for my eighth birthday they took me to Silverstone for courses 1 and 2 in karting.

When I began racing, naturally I wanted my own kart, and my parents were kind enough to buy me one, but then the problems started! Which series should I join? And was the kart I owned suitable? Having no racing background, my mum and dad had no idea which route to take. There was a myriad of kart series, and no obvious route to get into car racing. This is when *So, You Want to be a Racing Driver?* would have been very useful, but sadly a book of this sort wasn't available to me back then.

Luckily I was able to have some limited success, and aged 15 won a scholarship to race in the inaugural Formula BMW UK series, as my route into car racing. Still, there was no tried and tested route, even as I progressed through the ranks – should I do Formula BMW, or start with Formula Ford, should I then go straight to Formula 3 or Formula Renault – should I do British or Euro Series Formula 3, and so on. Some sort of guidance for someone new to motorsport would have been extremely beneficial, and I hope that those of you reading this book, who are about to embark on a new and exciting career into motor racing will reap the benefits.

My mum and I first met Leanne and her mother, a motorsport marshal at the time, at Oulton Park, (the passion clearly runs in the family). She has always supported me, and I am thrilled to offer the same support as she embarks on this exciting chapter as an author. On a side note, upon mentioning marshals I would also like to express thanks to all motorsport marshals for the work they do, enabling us drivers to go racing week after week.

Thank goodness Leanne succeeded in her chosen career. She has gathered vital experience and completed so much research during her time within the sport, which no doubt will help numerous young aspiring drivers to plot their route through the ranks of motorsport from a young age, to hopefully challenge me in my dotage.

Sam Bird

ABOUT THE AUTHOR

Leanne Fahy has worked in the motorsport industry in various guises for the last 14 years. Upon graduating from The University of Huddersfield in 2007, her first motorsport-related role was as a freelancer for *Autosport* magazine and *Motorsport News*, a position she fulfilled for the best part of a decade.

Since then, she has worked with different organisations, championships and series' (both two and four wheels), car and motor clubs, motor racing venues, teams and drivers, managing media and public relations campaigns. She also spent nine years working in an organisational and PR role for one of the UK's leading track day companies.

Now a director of her own motorsport-centred media company, 3 Phase Media Ltd, the knowledge and experience Leanne has gathered during her career has formed the basis for this book.

A NOTE FROM THE AUTHOR

Thank you for buying my book.

Making the decision to become a racing driver can be somewhat daunting, but I hope the information you will read in the following pages will make this step a little easier and prove to you just how achievable it is.

I hope you enjoy reading *So, You Want to Be A Racing Driver?* Hopefully, I will see you on-circuit sometime soon. Good luck.

DEDICATION

To my parents, for 35 years of love and support, for never questioning my career choice, and for driving a determined 15-year-old wannabe motorsport writer to races all over the country to pester racing drivers with my notebook and dictaphone. To Ryan and Stuart for always being there for their little sister, regardless of how far apart we may be. My grandparents, for continually showering us all with nothing but love, pride, and strength. To Mark, for all your love and encouragement, and for keeping me focused every day.

INTRODUCTION

It has occurred to me over the years just how elusive motorsport seems to be. Many thousands of people attend UK-based motor racing every season, and would love to become a racing driver themselves, but have no idea how to make that dream a reality, or just how achievable it can be.

In actual fact, it is much easier than it may seem. I will not create any illusions here, it is not going to be a cheap hobby, but you may be pleasantly surprised. As with many hobbies, it can be as affordable or as expensive as you make it, and it is certainly a lot easier to get into than you may realise. Whether you are a young karter or junior driver about to embark on a very exciting career in motorsport, someone who has finally decided to take the plunge, or even in the realms of retirement, motorsport knows no bounds – everyone is welcome.

Once the decision to become a competitor has been made there are many things to consider, but where do you start? *So, You Want to be a Racing Driver?* is designed to help guide you through each stage of the process, from making the initial decision right through to sitting on the grid for your first ever race. This book will fill in the sometimes daunting steps in-between.

The pages that follow will tell you everything you need to know, from setting a realistic budget, to applying for (and hopefully passing) your race or kart licence test, finding the right car for you, getting some seat time on-circuit, choosing which championship to join, and even the equipment you will need. The costs and prices quoted throughout the book were correct at time of writing, but please bear in mind that these will change over time, and should be checked online before setting a budget. As discussed throughout the book, the Covid-19 situation has altered the way certain activities are conducted, so please check with your club or the venue for the latest protocols when booking track days or race meetings, for instance.

There is plenty of information available, but this book intends to act as a one-stop guide; the only place you'll need to look to find everything you want to know.

CHAPTER 1

GETTING STARTED

THE RACING BUDGET
What to include when setting a budget

You have decided you want to start racing, that's step one, but one of the next questions you may ask is how expensive is it likely to be? As with any interest or hobby the cost is something to consider at the very beginning. Many of you may be under the impression that becoming a racing driver is far beyond your expectations and very much a pipe dream, but it may be easier to achieve than you think. I won't leave you under false pretences that motorsport is a bargain, but it can be accomplished in a cost-effective manner, you just need to know all of the options and what's available to you. The cost will differ depending on the route you take. Whether you opt for the karting route as an initial step into motorsport, or go straight into car racing, either as a junior or senior racer, I will guide you through the immediate process. So, let's get started straight away.

Kart racing budget

First stop: karting. Karting can be a bit of a minefield, as there are a great deal of options out there, for all ages. Many of today's professional and well-known racing drivers across all disciplines began their careers in the realms of karting. It is an extremely popular route to take, and a superb way to learn race craft and car control.

It may be the most common method to beginning a career in motorsport, but where does it sit on the affordability scale? Starting with a budget plan, the following list highlights the more important items that will need to be considered. This list is more applicable to those considering the more professional karting route, rather than joining a local indoor karting club, for instance. Much of this list is self-explanatory, but as someone new to karting, there may be some things you not have considered:

➤ Motorsport UK Go Karting Pack

> Competition licence (ARKS Licence)
> Kart
> Trailer
> Race kit
> Transponder
> Track days
> Test days
> Club membership
> Championship/Series registration
> Entry fees (per round)
> Mechanical equipment
> Medical or vision test (if applicable)

I will discuss each of these items in further detail throughout this book, including prices (at time of writing) where applicable, to give a general idea of how much you will need to allow for when planning your budget.

Car racing budget

Obviously in terms of car racing, the initial big expense will be your car, but there are a lot of other things to consider in your budget planning. Some of it is self-explanatory and may well be something you have already thought of, but as a new racing driver there will likely be a number of items you either have not thought of, or you haven't realised you will need. Your equipment list will most certainly grow as you work your way through your first season, when you discover more about what you need, and also when you see what other people in the paddock bring with them, but there are a few key items you will need when you begin. Make a list of everything you are likely to need and start to research prices; this will give an idea of expected expenditure and help to create an estimated budget for the season.

As a starting point I have listed some of the more important items you will need to consider within your budget plan for car racing. I will go into further detail on each of the items listed below throughout this book, including costs and where to find certain items:

> Motorsport UK Go Racing Pack
> Competition licence (ARDS Licence)
> Race car
> Trailer (and towing licence if applicable)
> Race kit
> Transponder
> Track days

- ➤ Test days
- ➤ Club membership
- ➤ Championship/Series registration
- ➤ Entry fees (per round)
- ➤ Mechanical equipment
- ➤ Medical and vision test (if applicable)

LICENCES

The process of acquiring a race licence is somewhat different to obtaining a road driving licence. Some of you will have already completed the process to gain a road driving licence, but young karters and junior racing drivers won't have had that opportunity yet. Although it's not described as a theory test, each person will be required to pass a written examination, as well as a practical test, in order to gain a competition licence, regardless of whether you are applying for a karting or car racing licence; however, that is where the similarities between road and race licences end. There are different competition licences available depending on the area of motorsport you wish to compete in. The various types of licence, along with the application process and associated costs will be discussed in more detail throughout this section.

This is also a good time to introduce you to Motorsport UK (MS UK). This is the governing body for all four-wheeled motorsport within the UK, and so all licences, regulations, and event permits are sanctioned by the Motorsport UK organisation. We will refer to Motorsport UK a great deal throughout this book, particularly during this section. Why not have a browse through the Motorsport UK website and familiarise yourself with the information it has available (www.motorsportuk.org). It's also worth familiarising yourself with the *Motorsport UK Yearbook* (or 'Blue Book' as it is more commonly known) as early as possible. The Blue Book, so named due to its blue cover, houses all rules, technical regulations and safety requirements relating to clothing, licence, equipment and car or kart for motorsport within the UK. These regulations are something you need to understand and also adhere to. You will receive your copy of the Blue Book within your Go Karting or Go Racing pack; however, you can also find a digital version of this on the Motorsport UK website. Karting also has its own dedicated yearbook, known as the Gold Book, that details all technical regulations specific to all classes and categories within karting. The Blue Book and Gold Book, together with *So, You Want to Be A Racing Driver?* is all the reading material you will need to accompany you on your quest for motorsport success.

2021 Application for Motorsport UK Competition Licence

motorsport UK

Get to the heart of the action quicker by having the following to hand:
- ✓ A 'passport style' image
- ✓ Your medical/vision test (if required - see section 4)
- ✓ Payment details

Read the 'What you need to know about your motorsport licence' booklet (available in the Resource Centre of **www.motorsportuk.org**) before filling in this form.

Any questions?

We are happy to help, call us on 01753 765050

Need your licence in a hurry?

- ☐ 3-hour processing, enclose an extra £115
- ☐ 3-day processing, enclose an extra £65

Did you know you may be able to apply for your licence online?

SOME OF OUR LICENCE HOLDER BENEFITS (Login to your member benefits portal online for more details)

halfords 10% off in-store

Wera Up to 10% off the full range of Wera tools

PIRELLI Up to £120 cash back on road tyres

SECTION 1A | YOUR DETAILS (Please write clearly in block capitals)

Surname _____

First name(s) _____

Gender ☐ Male ☐ Female   Date of birth __ / __ / __

Address _____

_____ Postcode _____

Phone number _____ Mobile _____

Email address _____

Nationality _____   Previous licence number ☐☐☐☐☐☐
(Non-British passport holders MUST enclose proof of residency in the UK e.g. a utility bill or bank statement)

Nationality and type of any other Competition Licence you hold _____

PLEASE ATTACH A PHOTOGRAPH HERE IF YOU HAVE NEVER SUPPLIED ONE TO US BEFORE, OR IF THERE HAS BEEN A MATERIAL CHANGE TO YOUR APPEARANCE (WRITE YOUR NAME AND DATE OF BIRTH ON ITS REVERSE).

SECTION 1B | PARENT, LEGAL GUARDIAN OR EMERGENCY CONTACT

⚠ If you are under 18, please provide the details of a parent or legal guardian. For over 18s, please provide details for your emergency contact.

Full name _____

Phone number _____ Email address _____

If your parent, legal guardian or emergency contact lives at a different address to you please provide below

_____

SECTION 1C | HOW DID YOU USE YOUR LICENCE?

Did you compete during 2020?   YES ☐ NO ☐

If 'Yes', please write the **number of events** you competed in next to each discipline below. If 'No', proceed to the next question below.

Autocross ____	Cross Country ____	Karting ____	Sprint ____
Autotest / Autosolo ____	Drag Racing ____	Rallycross ____	Trials ____
Circuit Racing ____	Hill Climb ____	Rallying ____	Other ____

Were you a member of a Club in 2020?   YES ☐ NO ☐

If 'Yes', please **write the number** of clubs you were a member of _____

t: +44 (0) 1753 765050   f: +44 (0) 1753 685426   w: motorsportuk.org

First page of Motorsport UK licence application form.

SO, YOU WANT TO BE A RACING DRIVER?

ARKS licence

Karting is well known for being the starting point for so many racing drivers, including many of the famous names we know from the world of motorsport. The Sennas and Buttons of the world began their motor racing career at a very young age amongst the karting ranks, proving the pedigree of drivers that karting can and has produced. There are countless local karting championships available for drivers of all ages; however, in terms of contesting a Motorsport UK sanctioned event, these are generally aimed at the younger members of the motorsport community. To compete in such an event, you will need a karting licence, or an ARKS licence.

What is an ARKS licence?

As mentioned above, to be eligible to race at a Motorsport UK karting event you will need the appropriate licence, in the case of karting this is an ARKS licence, approved by the Association of Racing Kart Schools (ARKS). Even as a young karter the correct licence is an absolute must to ensure you are legally allowed to compete.

Types of ARKS licence

There are different types of kart licence, depending on the discipline you wish to contest and also the level at which you compete. Differences arise when deciding whether to contest long circuit karting or short circuit karting, or whether you prefer endurance kart races, for instance. The difference in licences also comes into play with regard to the power of your kart and, more importantly, your age, as this will determine which class or championship you are eligible to take part in.

The types of kart licence available are listed below, together with the cost, and what events that particular licence entitles the holder to compete in. The prices detailed here are the licence renewal prices, the cost of your first licence will be detailed in the next section, 'How to get your ARKS licence':

Go Karting pack.

➤ Kart Clubman (Bambino) – £45
   Drivers can qualify for a Kart Bambino licence from the age of six years old
➤ Kart Clubman – £45
➤ Kart Interclub – £59
➤ Kart National – £89

In terms of age restrictions, you can apply for a Kart Race Long Circuit or Kart Endurance race licence from the age of 16. Drivers can apply for a Kart Race Short Circuit licence from the age of eight, whereas you need to be at least 11 years old to obtain a Kart Tyro licence.

How to get your ARKS licence

The first point of call when applying for your very first karting licence is to head to the Motorsport UK website to purchase a Go Karting starter pack. This pack is for those who are making their first application for a kart licence, not a Kart Clubman licence. The total cost of the pack alone is £59, inclusive of VAT, and it includes an application form for your licence, a booklet detailing the next steps to acquiring your licence, a Motorsport UK USB stick that includes the *Motorsport UK Yearbook* (the Blue Book), an instructional film that you will need to watch prior to completing the written portion of your examination, and a Motorsport UK keyring. The film will be used as part of your written assessment, so it is worth familiarising yourself with the content before booking your test. The cost of your first kart licence is included with the purchase of your Go Karting pack, so you won't have an additional licence fee on top of this. You will only need to pay for a licence separately when it comes to the renewal stage. For those karters under the age of 18, your Go Karting pack can also include a PG Entrant Licence if required, which your parent or guardian will need. This will be an additional £25 on top of your Go Karting pack.

Once you have received your pack you will need to book your ARKS test; this costs £98. You can book your test through one of the approved ARKS schools (listed below), or with the ARKS examiner at your local circuit.

During the exam you will be required to sit both a written and practical examination that will take place on the same day. In order to gain your kart race licence, you will need to pass both sections of the exam.

The ARKS schools listed here are all approved members of the Association of Racing Kart Schools (ARKS), and fully recognised by Motorsport UK. ARKS is responsible for not only carrying out the mandatory examination, but also for administering examiners. Only examiners approved by ARKS are qualified to assess drivers sitting their ARKS test.

The list of approved ARKS schools includes the following venues:

> Bayford Meadows
> Buckmore Park
> Castle Combe Circuit
> Clay Pigeon
> Nutts Corner
> Protrain Racing
> Three Sisters Kart Circuit
> Larkhall Karting
> Msport Karting
> Rye House
> Thruxton Circuit
> Tockwith Multi Drive Centre

Prior to booking your test, you can purchase a voucher online through the ARKS website. You will also need to purchase a suitable helmet; this will be discussed in more detail further on in this chapter, under the section 'Karting Equipment'.

Once you have booked your test and paid your £98, be aware that you may need to pay an additional fee if you do not have your own kart to use and need to hire one. The cost for kart hire will depend on who you book your test with. Whether this is the first time you have sat in a kart, or you are more well versed, the ARKS test is designed to suit all skill and experience levels. If you fail either part of the exam, both parts can be re-taken for a fee. The cost to re-sit your written examination is £50, whilst the cost for re-taking the practical portion of your exam is £60.

Drivers who are six years old and want to start karting can apply for their Go Karting pack. Once you have successfully completed your ARKS test, you can then apply for the Kart Interclub, or Bambino licence. Once armed with your Bambino licence, you will also receive a Bambino Record Card, on which you will collect signatures for the races you complete. Once you reach eight years old and you have collected enough signatures you can progress to the Cadet karting category.

Drivers looking to upgrade from a kart licence to a Race National licence can do so if they hold a Kart International A or B licence without further qualification. An ARDS race licence (explained below) will also permit you to enter a Long Circuit Kart event.

ARDS licence
What is an ARDS licence?
The Association of Racing Drivers Schools, or ARDS as it is commonly known, is the licence that car racing competitors will need if they choose the route of

circuit racing. Before being able to compete you will need the appropriate ARDS licence, of which there are different types and grades.

Go Racing pack.

Types of ARDS licence
There are different licences available, depending on the type of event you plan to contest. As a minimum, all competitors (and some passengers in the case of rallying) need to hold an RS Clubman licence to compete in a Motorsport UK permitted event. This was a new introduction to the Motorsport UK licensing structure in recent years, and it has been an excellent way to welcome new competitors into the sport. This licence is free of charge, saving you a significant cost; however, be aware that it is rather limited in terms of what it will allow you to contest. The RS Clubman licence is currently only applicable to those competing under a Motorsport UK Clubman permit in Autocross, Clubcross and Minicross events, Autotests and Autosolos, Trials, Cross Country events, as well as road and navigational rallies, therefore not applicable to those who want to compete in circuit racing.

There are various licence types and grades for those looking to compete in circuit racing. The different licence grades, from lowest to highest, are Clubman, Interclub, National and International. As you are just beginning your racing career it will be some time before you hold a higher grade of licence. It is also not a necessity that you upgrade your licence, this purely depends on the level you wish to compete at. If you plan to progress up the motorsport ladder to an international standard, you will need to follow the upgrade process. It is also worth noting that a higher licence grade will allow you to compete in lower permit events. For instance, you can compete in a UK club circuit racing event with an International race licence, and a race licence will enable you to compete in a speed event, such as a hillclimb or sprint, but it doesn't work the other way round, of course. You cannot compete in an international event with a Clubman Licence.

The different types of race licences are:

SO, YOU WANT TO BE A RACING DRIVER?

- **Race Club (Junior Championship – UK only)**

As a junior racing driver, you can only apply for the Race Club licence to start with; this can be done after your 14th birthday. Your licence application must be endorsed and submitted to Motorsport UK by a junior race championship organising club, such as those listed in Chapter Two. Your licence will state that it is only eligible for junior race formulae, and it will be held by the organising club of the championship you will contest for the duration of your junior racing career. Once you progress to a full race licence, you will keep hold of this yourself.

- **Race Club (UK only)**

This is the first race licence you will receive with your Go Racing pack, for those not categorised as junior drivers. To upgrade from the Race Club licence, you will need to receive six signatures for successfully completing races, and demonstrating you are a competent race driver. You can upgrade part way through the season, once you have received all six signatures, or you can wait until the normal renewal date (from 1st January).

- **Race National**

This is the licence most club level racing drivers will hold after losing their novice racing driver status. A Race National licence enables you to compete in car circuit racing in the UK. You can upgrade further to an International licence once you start to progress through the ranks.

- **Race International**

Drivers who hold a Race National licence can upgrade to either an International D or an International C licence. As with other upgrade processes, this can be done when you are ready to renew, or during the normal renewal date at the start of the year. Once you start applying for International race licences the renewal fee increases somewhat dramatically to reflect the level of competition.

There is also a Race National and International Truck licence, which is, quite obviously, for truck racing; however, this is unlikely to be the first stop on your motor racing journey. Those wanting to contest any of the rallying disciplines will need to follow the rallying licensing route, with your first licence being obtained through a Motorsport UK Go Rallying pack.

In terms of age restrictions, each discipline will project a specific minimum age for drivers. In terms of circuit racing, a junior racing driver can acquire a race licence from the age of 14. Junior drivers are aged between 14-16 years old. Once a driver reaches 16 years old, they will then apply for a normal (or senior) race licence that will open a number of doors in terms of which championships they can contest.

How to get your ARDS licence

The first step in applying for your ARDS licence, whether you are a junior driver (aged 14-16) or a senior competitor (16 years or over) is to purchase a Go Racing starter pack; this can be bought online through the Motorsport UK website.

The Go Racing pack costs £99, inclusive of VAT, and includes an application form for your first competition licence (race licence), a USB stick featuring the *Motorsport UK Yearbook* (the 'Blue Book'), an instructional film that you will need to watch ahead of the written portion of your examination, a booklet detailing the next steps you will need to take, and a Motorsport UK keyring. The cost of your first race licence is also included in the price of the Go Racing pack, so there are no extra costs upon completing your application.

To gain your race licence you will need to demonstrate you are capable of driving on-circuit consistently, in a safe and proficient manner, as well as proving you understand the basic on-track rules, for instance flag signals. You will complete two assessments as part of your test, with both taking place on the same day – a written, 'classroom' based assessment that will demonstrate your knowledge of driving on-circuit, flag signals and safety procedures, and a practical examination, which will take place on-circuit with a qualified ARDS instructor sat beside you. Although much of the written portion of your examination is common sense, for those bits you are not sure of, this information can be found in Section Q of your Blue Book.

You will need to purchase your Go Racing pack before you book your ARDS test, as you are required to take the pack with you on the day of your assessment. You may also need to pass a medical examination as part of the application process, to ensure you are fully fit to race. Applicants who are aged between 14 and 59, and applying for their first race or truck licence, will only be required to pass a vision test. However, if you are aged 60 or over and applying for your first race or truck licence, you will be required to pass a medical and a vision test. If you fall into the latter age range, again this is something you should complete before booking your ARDS test.

When the time comes to book your ARDS test, it will be through one of the registered schools, as listed on the ARDS website – www.ards.co.uk/schools. There may be different packages available to book, depending on your current experience. For example, Want2Race (discussed in more detail in Chapter Three) offers three ARDS packages: a basic package for those who already have track experience, offering the chance to gain your race licence with minimal instruction; an advanced package that provides more in-depth instruction prior to completing your test; and also a junior package for drivers aged 14-16. Other schools offer a set course and fee, so it depends which option suits you best. The good news is that the majority of ARDS schools have their own fleet of cars specifically for this purpose, so you don't need to worry about having a track car available.

You will find out on the day of your test whether you have passed or failed, so there will be no waiting nervously for another few days or weeks. Depending on which school you book with, ARDS tests may even take place on the same day as a normal track day. This will also give you vital experience of driving on-circuit whilst surrounded by other cars; something you will need to demonstrate you can manage during your practical examination. However, normally, you will find yourself on a day specifically dedicated to those who are there to gain their ARDS licence, so it should be a relatively straightforward experience.

Upon passing your ARDS test, your examining ARDS instructor will give you a stamped form to prove you have passed, that you will send to Motorsport UK to prove you have qualified for an ARDS licence. Motorsport UK will then post your new race licence to you. If you need your ARDS licence in a hurry, for example if you pass your test shortly before you are due to complete your first race, you can opt for a quicker processing time. Alternatively, contact Motorsport UK to explain the situation and it will issue you with a letter to give to your organising club, which will still allow you to compete.

As a newly-qualified racing driver you will initially be classified as a novice. Your novice branding will stay with you until you complete your first six races; after that you can rid yourself of that rookie status. In order to progress from being a novice, you need to collect six signatures on an upgrade card that is usually issued with your race licence. Before new Covid19 regulations came into force, you would fill in your details on the front and affix a passport photo to it, before handing it in to your organising race club prior to each race meeting. Following each of your races, your card would be signed by a club official, providing you have completed each race, and in a safe manner. Handing in your upgrade card would normally be carried out during the sign-on process; however, because of Covid19 restrictions, the sign-on process for race meetings has changed (discussed in more depth in Chapter Four), and that in turn has affected the upgrade system. Under new procedures you can download your upgrade card from the Motorsport UK website, then, to get it signed and updated, you will need to find the results from each of your races, print them and post them, along with your upgrade card to Motorsport UK. Your card will then be signed, updated and your novice status will diminish. Make sure you affix a passport photograph, or your upgrade card may be turned away.

An example of an upgrade card, for use when upgrading to higher level licences.

If you are unable to complete six races in quick succession, you can speed up the process of collecting your six signatures by completing a day as a motorsport marshal. Marshals are volunteer officials, who stand trackside during races, recognisable by their distinctive orange overalls. Very highly trained for all eventualities, motorsport marshals are the first on scene following an incident on track. Drivers can receive a signature towards their race licence upgrade by spending a day on the bank. It also presents you with a very different perspective of the circuit, which can be helpful.

The costs associated with gaining your ARDS licence include:

➤ Go Racing pack – £99 (incl VAT)
➤ ARDS Test – from £200 (prices differ depending on the school and package)

As mentioned, those looking to start their competitive racing career in events such as Autotests and trial events can do so with the RS Clubman licence, although there is no need to sit an examination as part of the application process. If you wish to upgrade to the RS Clubman National licence, the Association of Hillclimb and Sprint Schools (AHASS) offers a written examination that counts as a signature towards your licence upgrade.

If you want to begin your journey in hillclimbing or sprinting, you will first need to be a member of a motor club recognised by Motorsport UK. There are plenty of clubs that organise hillclimbing and sprinting events across the UK, and no doubt there will be at least one fairly local to you. Once you are a member, you will also need to apply for an RS Interclub licence; this will entitle you to enter a road legal vehicle in suitable classes at a hillclimb or sprint event.

You can upgrade your RS Interclub licence to an RS National licence upon receiving six signatures. As mentioned above, you can receive one signature by attending the AHASS and by sitting and passing an examination, other signatures must be obtained from the Clerk of the Course after completing six Interclub hillclimb or sprinting events. These events must take place at a minimum of two different venues.

Licence renewals

With the cost of your first race licence included with your Go Karting or Go Racing pack you don't need to worry about that for a little while. However, your licence will need to be renewed prior to each season. If you let your licence lapse for a couple of years without renewing it, you may need to re-sit the written portion of the ARDS test. This will be determined by Motorsport UK. Race licences tend to start on 1st January and expire on 31st December, regardless of when you purchase your pack.

January is often a busy time for Motorsport UK, as licence renewals come in by the thousands. Processing time usually takes around 15 days if done by post, or 10 days if you apply online, so make sure to send in your renewal application in plenty of time. If you do this at the start of the year it allows plenty of time for processing before the start of the season; this usually starts around the end of March or the beginning of April. If you are in a rush for your licence to come back, you can request express handling, which costs £65 for three days or £115 for three hours.

In terms of licence renewal costs for racing and karting disciplines, the prices are as follows:

Race licence renewals:
➤ Race National – £155
➤ Race Club (UK Only) – £99
➤ Race Club (Junior Championships, UK Only) – £99

Kart licence renewals:
➤ Kart National – £89
➤ Kart Inter Club (UK Only) – £59
➤ Kart Clubman (UK Only) – £45
➤ Kart Clubman Bambino (UK Only) – £45
➤ Entrant PG licence (for drivers under the age of 18) – £25

Those competing in long circuit karting will need to book a vision test from the age of 14.

If you wish to upgrade your race licence, and your upgrade card is completed as instructed with a passport-sized photograph attached to it, this can be sent back to the Motorsport UK licensing department, together with your licence renewal form.

Although you may not have needed a full medical when applying for your first licence, those who have reached the age of 60, 65, 70, 72, 74 or 75 since applying for their previous licence will need to book a medical examination as part of their licence renewal.

RACE EQUIPMENT

Moving on to race equipment, there are a number of items you will need, even as a novice karter or racing driver, and other equipment that may become more useful as your racing career develops. Once you surround yourself with fellow competitors, your list of key items will gradually expand as you see what other people are using. Once you borrow something from a fellow competitor more than two or three times, it is usually worth investing in that piece of equipment yourself, but ensuring that you begin with the essentials will be enough to see you through your first few race meetings, at least.

In terms of race clothing, as a minimum you will need a race helmet, neck protection, fire resistant overalls, gloves and boots, each of must meet an approved standard. Clothing and safety regulations will differ between karting and car racing, although most of the outlets I mention in this section will sell equipment for both. I will get to the safety checks and scrutineering process for your equipment shortly, but you can check the required standard of your race kit in sections Q and K of the Blue Book.

As well as helping to decide what constitutes an essential item for your kit bag, the following section will also divulge the best places to buy everything, from fire-resistant underwear (yes, that's right, fire-resistant underwear is a must) to your race suit, gloves, boots, helmet, and so much more.

Essential race kit

Before diving in and purchasing everything you think you are likely to need, it's best to do a bit of research. As well as ensuring you are kitted out in the safest gear, always be mindful of exactly what you will need, and of course, the cost. I appreciate you may be working to a particular budget, and although safety equipment is not something that should be compromised, it does not mean you have to purchase the most expensive gear. Whilst doing your research, check the safety standard of your particular helmet brand, for instance: there will be plenty of reviews available. Also pay close attention to the items you are looking to buy, as some helmets and race suits may be suitable for karting but not car racing and vice versa. I will discuss details about the standard set for clothing and equipment in this section, although you can also find this in your Blue Book. A little research in the first instance will help you gather a better idea of your budget for the season. There's no denying that your kit list will grow as you progress, and that applies to karters and car racers, but it's important to establish your starting point.

First of all, be aware that there are certain safety regulations to follow with regard to your race kit. You may or may not know that all race clothing and safety equipment must adhere to a certain safety standard, set out by Motorsport UK. Some items in your kit bag may include an expiration date. Please take note, as out-of-date or damaged equipment, or items deemed to be unsafe, could be confiscated during scrutineering checks, potentially threatening your permission to race.

Prior to 2020 and the Covid-19 pandemic, all of your equipment, from race clothing to your car, would have been checked at each round during the scrutineering process, both to ensure you have the correct equipment and that it is safe to use. However, this is one of the many things that has had to change during the 2020 season, in order to minimise contact with one another. With safety at the forefront of the sport, Motorsport UK adopted a new procedure, in which competitors complete an online declaration prior to each race meeting, detailing the specification of everything from their race helmet to their fire extinguisher, to confirm their equipment is safe to use. Following this, at many club level race meetings, a small percentage of drivers will also then be selected at random to be physically checked by a scrutineer at the respective event. These spot checks are in place to ensure drivers adhere to important safety regulations, whilst still maintaining limited contact between people. Those who have been selected at random for a spot check will be notified in advance.

Please find below your essential equipment check list. Although the type of items on the list may differ slightly between karting and car racing, the basic list is essentially the same for both. You will soon get into a routine of what you need for a track or test day, and what you need for a race meeting, which may differ slightly. Use the list below to make sure you never forget an item. I will discuss each of the items in this list in more detail throughout this section for anyone with further queries:

➤ Helmet
➤ HANS device (for car racing rather than karting)
➤ Fireproof overalls
➤ Fireproof (Nomex) underwear
➤ Gloves
➤ Wrist restraints (if racing in an open top car)
➤ Race boots
➤ Neck collar (for karting only)

A word of advice, always be prepared with your full safety equipment, even on a track or test day. Although car-to-car contact is highly unlikely on a track day, other incidents can occur, whether forced by a mechanical issue or driver error. Always be prepared.

Where to buy your race kit

There are plenty of places to buy your racing equipment, from clothing to tools, with prices differing between different outlets. As with the majority of things these days, there is a great deal of variety available online. Although your product research is easily completed online, when it comes to purchasing this is often best carried out in store, where possible.

Let's start with clothing and safety equipment. As you will have gathered by now, research is key when it comes to motorsport, and this particularly applies to your safety equipment. Before rushing to buy the first helmet and race suit you see, it is important to do your research. Prices and sizes will differ greatly between different brands and outlets. Although visiting a shop in person may be somewhat more difficult due to time constraints, it is worth trying things on where possible before you commit to buying, particularly when it comes to your helmet. Your race helmet is something that needs to fit perfectly, for one thing to ensure it is comfortable, but more importantly the correct size will ensure maximum protection.

Karting equipment

The approved standard for helmets and overalls with regard to karting is set out in the Blue Book, under sections K and U. When purchasing your helmet, ensure it is suitable for karting, as regulations will differ to that of car racing. As well as conforming to the correct standard you must ensure your helmet is the correct fit, it can be securely fastened and is in good condition. Before completing your ARKS test make sure you have a suitable helmet; you will need this during the practical section of your examination. If you have booked your ARKS test and you are under 15 years of age, the only helmet standard you will be able to use is a SNELL CMR2016, or the CMS equivalent. All helmet standards are set out below, with different regulations and standards depending on your age. Make sure your helmet is a karting helmet, not a motorcycle helmet, as this will not be eligible.

Helmet standards as determined in the Blue Book for national karting events and drivers over 15 years old must adhere to the following:

➤ SNELL K2010 (Not valid after 31st December 2023)
➤ SNELL K2015
➤ SNELL – FIA CMR2007
➤ SNELL – FIA CMS2007

> SNELL – FIA CMR2016
> SNELL – FIA CMS2016

For kart drivers under the age of 15, Cadet and Bambino drivers, the weight of the helmet is also important, and must not exceed 1550g. Helmet standards for drivers in this group are as follows:

> SNELL – FIA CMR2007
> SNELL – FIA CMS2007
> SNELL – FIA CMR2016
> SNELL – FIA CMS2016

In terms of karting specific regulations, all drivers are required to wear a full-face helmet during all track activity, as well as display a Motorsport UK helmet approval sticker, which can be purchased from Motorsport UK and costs £2.50. Once your helmet has been approved this sticker should be affixed to your helmet in a specific location either by a scrutineer, by Motorsport UK or by a selected manufacturer. For karting approved helmets, the correct approval sticker is green or yellow. Helmets should always be accompanied by a fire resistant balaclava.

Moving onto overalls, again there are specific requirements your suit must meet to deem it worthy of being accepted by a scrutineer, with slightly different regulations depending on whether you are contesting long circuit karting or short circuit karting. Regardless of circuit type, your race suit must carry a thickness of 1.2mm. To make it easier to find the correct suit, have a look for level one or two on the collar of the suit, this will be located next to the CIK/FIA manufacturing date range.

All drivers contesting long circuit karting events must wear a leather race suit, or a suit approved for long circuit karting by Motorsport UK. Those opting to compete in short circuit karting events must wear either a leather race suit, or suits that bear a recognised CIK homologation to the following standard:

> No 2001-1
> No 2013-1, level 1 or 2

Next, you will need race boots and gloves. People often ask if they can just wear normal trainers instead of race boots, but this is not permitted, for both practicality and safety. Not only are race boots a more suitable alternative to normal shoes or trainers due to the fact that they are narrow and thin soled, and so help with maximum pedal control, but they also cover and protect your ankles. Gloves should be a complete item, not open backed, for instance, to ensure complete coverage and so they protect your hands as best they can.

Other important items to consider having in your kit bag come in the form of body and neck protection. You may see other karters wearing a rib protector; as the name suggests this provides a level of protection to your ribs in the event of an incident. Those available range from a rib protection waistcoat at the lower end of the price range (£48), to carbon rib protectors, priced between £200-300. In terms of neck safety, a neck collar will add an extra level of protection whilst on-circuit, should you need it. Neck collars, the karting equivalent of a HANS device (a piece of equipment used by drivers in car racing and rallying), range from £40 to £80, depending on the product you choose and the retailer. Knee and elbow pads may also be useful for karting, and although they are not an essential piece of kit, you may prefer to have that extra bit of safety on your side.

In terms of undergarments, fire resistant tops, trousers and socks are all available, to offer as much protection as possible. You will find race clothing retailers in abundance with a quick Google search, but take time to assess the products available, to make sure they comply with the regulations. To make it easier, I have discussed a number of the main retailers further on in this chapter.

Car racing equipment
The type of necessary race clothing for drivers contesting car racing is largely the same as that for karting,although the regulations will differ slightly.

Starting with your race helmet, in the same manner as karting, you need to ensure it fits you properly, it fastens securely, and it is in a strong, functional condition. For all national Motorsport UK events, the necessary standards for your helmet include:

➤ FIA 8860-2010
➤ FIA 8859-2015
➤ SNELL SA2010 (Not valid after 31st December 2023)
➤ SNELL SA2015 (Not valid after 31st December 2026)
➤ SNELL SAH2010 (Not valid after 31st December 2023)
➤ SNELL SA2020

As with karting, your helmet will need to carry a Motorsport UK approval sticker. There is a charge of £2.50 for this sticker, and it is available from Motorsport UK. The sticker can only be affixed by a nominated scrutineer, Motorsport UK or a designated manufacturer. Unlike karting, the approval sticker for all other disciplines is blue, so ensure you are sporting the correct label. Your helmet and HANS device will be checked by a scrutineer at the start of the year, and if missing, this sticker will be applied to both then.

Something that was not mentioned in the karting equipment information is a HANS (Head and Neck Support) device, but this is part of your compulsory equipment for other disciplines, particularly car racing. As the name suggests, the HANS device is a type of head support that provides an extra level of protection to your head and neck. It was originally designed in the early 1980s and has developed further during the last four decades. Made primarily of carbon fibre material, the purpose of the device is to prevent the head making forceful, whipping movements in the event of a crash. Once in position, the device is tethered to the helmet, by a post on each side, to ensure restricted head movements in the event of an accident. Although head movements are restricted when necessary, your range of movements aside from that and field of vision remains unaffected.

After becoming a mandatory piece of equipment in Formula One in 2003, followed by the World Rally Championship and the popular Australian V8 Supercar Series in 2005, this filtered down to grassroots motorsport shortly afterwards and is now one of the most important items in your kit bag.

There are different types of head and neck restraints available, depending on your personal preference and comfort. The most popular choice tends to be the HANS device, that sits on your shoulders and behind your neck. An alternative mechanism is the Hybrid Sport Frontal Head Restraint (FHR) device, from Simpson Racing, worn around your shoulders, (like a waistcoat, basically) and fastened around your chest. There is now also a new design of the FHR device, designed specifically for female racing drivers, a superb step in the right direction. As with other FHR devices, the female-centred model is also available from Simpson Racing. The original HANS and Hybrid Sport devices are some of the only head restraint devices that have passed the sanctioned standard, and two main options for drivers racing in Motorsport UK sanctioned events.

In the case of both implements, your seatbelts must sit on top of the device straps and attach to your helmet. You will notice your helmet will have posts on each side, for your HANS device to click into. This part is important to ensure the device will properly support your head and neck.

As with other items in your kit bag, your race suit must adhere to a certain standard. It must be flame resistant and cover your body from ankle to wrist to neck, to ensure you have no skin exposed at all. Your balaclava will also cover any skin that may be showing around your neck. Acceptable standards of suits for racing must fall into one of the following categories:

➤ FIA 8856-2018
➤ FIA 8856-2000

Your suit may become unsuitable following damage or excessive wear. As with many garments, this is inevitable over time; however, other factors can contribute to your race suit becoming unacceptable, such as over- or incorrect washing, damaged or ripped seams and worn patches. I'm sure you will have grasped by now that different disciplines must follow different standards, so be sure to double-check your race suit if you plan to contest something other than car racing.

Race boots are another important item in your kit bag. Although mandatory for circuit racing they have multiple benefits, as opposed to wearing your normal footwear. First of all, race boots include a protective layer of fire-retardant Nomex material as an extra level of protection. Additionally, as previously mentioned, their thin soles help to ensure good pedal control, and maximise throttle and braking opportunities. There are copious varieties of race boots on the market, usually sporting either a leather or suede finish. Some have a Velcro strap across the ankle to provide a bit of extra support. Although the basic concept is the same, there are a great deal of styles and variations available. You may even want to colour coordinate your race boots with your race suit, gloves or helmet; that's when it gets really serious.

As with karting, you will also need to wear a flame-resistant balaclava underneath your helmet, and appropriate gloves. Flame-resistant undergarments, such as a long-sleeved Nomex top, socks and underwear, are also very important and definitely worth having in your kit bag.

Safety certainly comes first when climbing into a race car, and the equipment designed to protect you should be the best it can be. The likelihood is you may not need to test just how safe your equipment is, but on the off-chance you do, you want to feel confident that it will do the job it's designed to do.

Where to find your race kit

One of the most popular sources, and one you are likely to hear mentioned repeatedly both in and away from the paddock, is Demon Tweeks. Founded in 1971, Demon Tweeks has a wealth of knowledge and experience behind its brand and is very much at the forefront when it comes to motorsport equipment. Supported by a strong online presence, the Demon Tweeks online shop makes your motorsport shopping task a very easy one, especially once you know what you want. If you prefer to shop in person, you can visit Demon Tweeks at its Wrexham base. Catering for all disciplines, including, of course, karting and circuit racing, this really is a one-stop-shop for everything from clothing to tools and workshop equipment.

It is also worth keeping an eye out for the renowned Demon Tweeks 10% discount: once you start interacting with others in the paddock, you will undoubtedly hear about this. Some motorsport clubs offer this incentive to its members upon signing up to race with them; however, you could also be eligible by signing up to become a member of Demon Tweeks. When you begin buying your race kit, every bit of discount you can save will certainly help your budget. Additionally, Demon Tweeks offers a sponsorship scheme. Applications are accepted from racing drivers who hold a valid race licence and who are competing in some Motorsport UK events. If you are accepted to the sponsorship scheme, you will be entitled to the following benefits, designed to help with the associated costs of racing:

> ➤ Free membership
> ➤ Free phone number direct to the Demon Tweeks sales team – exclusive to members
> ➤ Free help and advice from knowledgeable staff
> ➤ Easy online ordering
> ➤ Updates on the latest products and innovations on the Demon Tweeks website
> ➤ Free sticker pack for all sponsorship scheme members, to ensure your car looks the part
> ➤ The chance to win multiple £150 vouchers claimed throughout the season

Although the scheme is limited to 2000 members each year, it is open to drivers from all UK motorsport disciplines, such as circuit racing, karting, rallying, hillclimbing, auto grass events, rallycross, oval racing, sprinting, drifting, drag racing, truck racing and sim racing. Applications can be made via the Demon Tweeks website.

Another motorsport retailer worth investigating is Grand Prix Racewear. Very driver focused, Grand Prix Racewear is another experienced outlet; after over 30 years in the business it has established itself as the UK's premier racewear emporium. Based at the Silverstone Circuit complex, Grand Prix Racewear, or GPR as it is more commonly known in the paddock, caters for all manner of racing drivers, from karting through to the top flight of the sport, with a varied price list to match. Although you can visit the GPR shop, the company also has a strong online presence, for those more well versed in online shopping. I purchased my own race boots from GPR whilst working at a Silverstone race meeting one weekend, very conveniently, and so I can highly recommend it for a thorough and helpful service.

Grand Prix Racewear, as the name quite clearly suggests, is heavily centred around clothing, with a focus on race suits, race boots, helmets, and a variety of other motorsport themed clothing. However, it still features a selection of motorsport equipment, such as seats and harnesses, pit equipment, car preparation and setup apparatus, steering wheels and workshop essentials. GPR have separate sections for circuit racing and karting, with a large range of items available in both categories, from clothing to safety equipment and kit bags.

WASPP, a new name in the motorsport equipment industry in 2020, has rapidly built a strong presence and reputation for itself in the paddock and beyond. WASPP sells everything you could need, from gaffer tape to race suits, and supplies everything for the driver, the car and the workshop. Although the WASPP name was a new venture in 2020, the personnel behind the brand are certainly experienced within the sport. Run by husband and wife team, Jay and Kate Shepherd, and business partner Edward Worthington, the team has been involved in motorsport for many years in many guises. Jay and Kate also run a race team themselves, so they are well-versed in knowing exactly what you are likely to need during a race meeting and back home in your garage. As well as supplying motorsport equipment, WASPP sponsored a number of championships and drivers during the 2020 season, further cementing its position in the industry.

Torq Racewear is another brand that comes highly recommended. Designed in the UK, Torq Racewear also offers everything from Nomex undergarments to gloves and suits, for both karting and circuit racing. Its competitive prices means Torq is a popular name in the UK club motor racing scene. It also sells team wear, so when you get to the point of having a team of people helping you run your race car, whether friends or family, you can all look the part in your professional team clothing. Armed with distributors all over the world, Torq has a very strong presence within the industry.

Vital Equipment is a name you will likely become familiar with once you are more involved in the motorsport industry, whether you hear it from fellow competitors or the company's presence in the motorsport paddock. Heavily involved in the sport, as the name suggests, Vital Equipment provides all manner of supplies needed to compete. From essential racewear, such as helmets, race overalls, HANS devices, gloves, boots, and Nomex underwear, to safety equipment, including fire extinguishers and extinguisher equipment. You can also find all you need for vehicle preparation and workshop consumables, to fuel and oil handling essentials. Vital Equipment is another one-stop shop for everything you need to make your motor racing journey that bit easier.

GSM Performance is another retailer that stocks a huge range of products, from all manner of mandatory racewear to sports seats and performance brakes. Based in Nottinghamshire, GSM Performance provides expert advice as you browse its vast collection, as well as competitive prices for racing essentials.

Race Cars Direct (www.racecarsdirect.com) is a popular port of call when searching for everything you could need in motorsport. Whether you are buying or selling, and whether you are a team, driver or fan, you will find a category that fits the bill. Purchasing a car or kart from Race Cars Direct is discussed later, but with regard to everything else you could possibly need, it is a useful hub. Categories included on the Race Cars Direct website include:

- ➤ Race cars – for every discipline imaginable
- ➤ Race and rally parts
- ➤ Race car transport – from single car trailers to race trucks
- ➤ Rally cars
- ➤ Drives available – either from teams looking to fill a seat or drivers looking for a car to hire
- ➤ Pit equipment
- ➤ Workshop equipment and supplies
- ➤ Karts and parts
- ➤ Performance cars
- ➤ Classic road cars
- ➤ Race meetings, track and test days
- ➤ Clubs and championships
- ➤ Memorabilia
- ➤ Motorsport news and product reviews
- ➤ Motorsport careers

The variety of outlets available shows how useful it can be to complete thorough research prior to purchasing your race kit and essential equipment, with prices differing somewhat between the various retailers. As well as the retailers mentioned here, there is also the option to visit the manufacturers directly. Brands such as Arai, Sparco and OMP, for example, each have their own online shops, with a great deal of choice on their respective websites. Knowledgeable staff will also be able to help guide you towards the best product for you. Again, as you would expect, prices will differ between the manufacturers and the various retailers, so be sure to add this to your research list. Although be warned, once you start browsing website after website, your racing wish list may rapidly expand.

You will find that most circuits have their own dedicated shop on site, with most selling equipment from essential car stickers, such as novice crosses, extinguisher and electrical markers, to driver kit and even axle stands. Just be aware that some circuit shops may be more fan than driver focused, selling circuit memorabilia rather than race suits, for instance. Be sure to check this out before relying on being able to top up your kit bag whilst at the circuit.

Another option has always been the Autosport International Racing Car Show that takes place at the National Exhibition Centre (NEC) in Birmingham in January each year. Spread across four days, this is seen as the start of the racing season for many, and one of the places to find the majority of the equipment you will need for the season ahead. The large halls of the NEC are packed with leading professionals from the motorsport industry, from racing clubs, championships, and series, to engineering, mechanical and safety equipment suppliers. The show also acts as a central hub for those wanting to meet like-minded individuals, especially useful if you are new to the sport. Motorsport UK also usually has a presence at the show, which is extremely helpful if you have any queries.

As with anything, you can always find more variety on content and pricing with more online research, but the above options are a good starting point. If you are a social media user, it is worthwhile joining pages or groups specific to your championship. Although some equipment, such as helmets, race suits and boots will need to be purchased new, you can often find some secondhand equipment and tools from your fellow competitors.

CHAPTER 2

WHAT TO RACE AND WHERE

KARTING

Karting is a great way to break into the motorsport bubble, whether that's as a youngster taking your first steps into the sport, or as an adult who has joined your local club and wants to take it further. Regardless of your age, it can be a superb way to begin your motorsport journey, as well as to develop race craft. You will learn skills and techniques behind the wheel of a kart that will undoubtedly benefit you in a race car, if you decide to progress along that route. During this chapter, we will explore the options available for those looking at the karting route, from the actual kart itself through to the various categories, championships and clubs available to you, and how to progress from karting, should you want to take that next step.

Although there are countless opportunities to join the karting fraternity out there, it's a fairly simple process for those who are new to the discipline. It is extremely accessible, and a great deal of fun, regardless of age. Being based in the UK means we are extremely lucky when it comes to karting, as there are currently over 150 kart circuits in existence, from indoor venues for the more informal competition, to purpose-built outdoor facilities that play host to all manner of international karting competition.

The kart

So, first step, the kart. As discussed in Chapter 1, if you decide to purchase a kart outright this is the largest outgoing cost associated with your chosen discipline, but also it is the most important cost, obviously. If you do not want to commit to buying a kart, many circuits will have various hire packages available. Although this might not be such a large financial commitment, it is still a cost you will need to factor into your budget. It is also worth comparing both options, for instance if you intend to complete a full season of karting, it may not work out much cheaper to hire a kart; however, it depends on whether consumables such as fuel and tyres are included in your hire package.

As a young karter, your age will likely determine the club or championship you initially decide to join. In turn, that will dictate the type of kart you get, so hopefully this should be a fairly straightforward process for you.

In terms of technical regulations, all karts will need to abide by a strict set of policies, however there may be supplementary regulations within your chosen club or championship. As you would expect, your kart needs to be presented as safe to use, with all components being capable of achieving the speeds expected when on-circuit. Your kart must be in a suitable condition to be checked and approved by a scrutineer at any point. The regulations you can expect to see will refer to the dimensions of your kart, the flooring, its suspension, wheels, tyres, brakes, steering, sub axles, seating, pedals and exhausts. There will also be restrictions on the type of fuel you will be allowed to use. Regulations are in place to ensure a level playing field for all competitors and must be followed to the letter. For more information on the specific policies in place, all details can be found under Section U of your Blue Book.

One final expense to mention when it comes to buying or renting a kart is insurance. There are plenty of companies in the insurance industry who specialise in motorsport specific policies, whether it is for karting, car racing or track days. However, it is one of those things that you don't always have to have in order to race.

If you are hiring a kart, either insurance will be included in the price of the hire, or you will have an option for insurance. In this instance, it is always worth taking the insurance option. You won't plan to have an incident on-circuit during a race, however sometimes it is out of your control if caused by a third party. It could be a case of wrong place, wrong time for you, and before you know it you are caught up in someone else's accident and left with a sizeable repair bill. Although there is a high chance you could pay for your insurance and never need it, it's more for peace of mind, and to protect your racing budget should the worst happen. Being faced with an excess to pay, rather than the full repair bill is a much better position to be in.

If you are buying your own kart, again, insurance is a personal choice. I know of plenty of drivers who do not opt for insurance cover and are happy to take that chance. Policies will cover you for a variety of things, not just accident cover but also public liability cover as well. Insurance cover will also help protect you in the event your kart or trailer is stolen from your storage location.

Whatever the track action you are competing in, if you would like to consider karting insurance, there are a number of companies who specialise in varying levels of cover, specific to the karting industry, such as:

➤ MIS Motorsport (a very well known company in the motorsport industry)
➤ Sports Cover Direct
➤ Peacock Insurance

➤ Primo Plc
➤ Park Insurance

As with all insurance policies it is worth shopping around to see which level of cover best suits you.

Where to find your kart

When it comes to actually finding your kart, there are countless directories to try. Once again, this is where some thorough research comes into play, and as ever the internet is a wonderful tool.

One of the first ports of call for aspiring drivers looking for a kart is Race Cars Direct. With various sections for race cars, transporters, pit equipment, memorabilia and so much more, it is a central hub for those who are buying and selling. Its Karts and Parts category will come in very handy when you start the search. With different sections for those who are selling and those who are buying karts and subsequent parts, you will likely find something useful.

You will certainly find karts for sale in more than just one place, so be sure to widen your search parameters. Following a brief Google search, I was able to find a significant number of karts for sale, each matching different classes, some on eBay, and some from respected karting teams. If you are looking at purchasing a secondhand kart, which you most likely will be, other options to try include karting magazines or speaking to your local kart clubs. Once you decide to start karting, the best course of action is to familiarise yourself with your local karting scene. This may include going along to some race meetings and getting to know the club officials and some of the other drivers. As well as immersing yourself in the karting scene in person, it is useful to start looking at karting magazines and perhaps even join some Facebook karting groups. This will enable to you get to know the right people, as well as help when you are trying to find a kart or other equipment to buy. Be as prepared as you can be.

The other option is to hire a kart, either from one of the many professional kart teams, or from one of the circuits. Many of the circuits offer an arrive-and-drive package, or even arrive-and-drive championships. This could be advantageous for those with limited storage space at home. It also negates the need to allow for a trailer to transport your kart to each race. Obviously owning your own kart has major plus points, you know exactly what work goes into maintaining it, and you have it at your disposal as and when you want to race. There are certainly advantages and disadvantages for the buying versus hiring dispute; these largely depend on your budget, storage and transport options.

Whoever you are buying or hiring from, I can almost guarantee when you find a kart you are interested in, you will search back through its race history, to find results from previous races. Although I know of so many drivers who have done this, do not read too much into past results. It is comforting to know you are purchasing a race- or championship-winning kart; however, there are a number of external factors that contribute to the performance of a vehicle; different drivers make a significant difference for one.

The trailer

If you are planning to buy your own kart rather than go for a hire package, another item you will need is a trailer. The benefit of transporting a kart around over a race car is that it is much smaller; therefore your trailer can be smaller.

More than likely you will purchase a trailer secondhand, which is a perfectly acceptable option. As with buying a kart or car, it is best to shop around to ensure you select the best trailer for your needs.

Whilst car trailers tend to come in a variety of options, from open trailers to different types of covered trailer, kart trailers usually come as a covered, box style trailer. This offers maximum protection for your kart and can also act as a shelter whilst at race meetings. Prices for trailers vary depending on where you get them from and the quality of the equipment. If you do decide to trailer your own kart, or your parent or guardian does, you will also need to arrange for storage and a suitable tow vehicle.

Due to the somewhat compact size of a kart, trailers can sometimes be designed to cater for two or three karts, so you may well be able to share transport with one or two fellow competitors. This will be much cheaper than buying a trailer outright, as well as help with any storage concerns. However, remember this will mean you may not always have full access to it should you want to go somewhere different to compete or test

Other essential equipment

You are now armed with your full race kit and safety equipment; you have your kart and your transport is sorted in the form of a trailer: what else could you possibly need? This section lists additional items you may not have thought of, but that could be quite essential.

First of all, a pop-up awning. I mentioned above that your trailer could double up as shelter for those days of questionable weather. However, an alternative, especially if you are hiring a kart and don't have a trailer, is a pop-up awning, particularly one with sides. This will act as a shelter, and will also provide an extra degree of protection for your kart.

This may be simple, and quite possibly something you have already thought of, but a table and chairs will be very useful, as well as a kettle, tea and coffee making facilities and some cold drinks. A good quantity of water will be very welcome for drivers as they finish their heats or races. With that, you will also need some sort of electrical connection. Most circuits provide electric hook-up points that you can connect your own cable to. An alternative to this is to ensure you have access to a generator. Whether you hire one or share one with a fellow competitor, it is a very useful piece of equipment to have, especially for those times when the circuit does not facilitate the use of electricity.

Categories, championships and clubs

You will have noticed I have referred to long circuit karting and short circuit karting, but what's the difference? Both are outdoor events, but short circuit karting takes place on a circuit less than 1500 metres in length. Short circuit courses tend to be purpose-built for karting events, and host races for both gearbox and non-gearbox karts. Long circuit karting takes place on a circuit longer than 1500 metres. These events lend themselves to a more common motorsport event, taking place on some of the main motorsport circuits, rather than kart-specific venues. Usually only open to gearbox kart races, such as Superkarts, you will often find these types of races alongside other general motorsport events, such as club level car racing.

Karting categories

Now we have established that, let's move on to the various classes. Starting at the very beginning we have Bambino karting, designed for six- to eight-year-olds. To be a Bambino karter you must be signed off by a qualified ARKS instructor or examiner as competent prior to being allowed to compete in a Motorsport UK event. Since 2018, Bambino karters from the age of seven have been eligible to compete in Motorsport UK championship competitions; however, in order to achieve this, drivers must have competed in at least six Motorsport UK time trial events.

In terms of race format, Bambino karting events either run as a time trial, with drivers released at set intervals, or as a Motorsport UK sanctioned race. The Bambino class is relatively new, however there are plenty of opportunities to get involved in the class at some of the approved centres throughout the UK; this will be discussed in the next section.

Organised on specially approved mini circuits, this is the ideal setting for young karters to learn and navigate their way through their first kart competition. All drivers are classified as either bronze, silver or gold graded competitors, and as a nice reward each driver will receive a certificate of attendance. Bambino karting is designed to allow karters to compete from the earliest age possible, and is a good way to determine when a driver is ready to apply for a kart race licence. To ensure everyone has the same opportunity to succeed, the only kart allowed in Bambino karting is the Comer C50, which runs with a 50cc engine. Engine identification seals are in place on all Bambino class karts, to reduce the risk of tuning and engine work.

Once a driver reaches the ripe old age of eight, if they opt to continue on their karting journey, they graduate to the Cadet category. Designed for karters aged eight to 12, the Cadet category is quite a step up. As well as complying with the age range for Cadet karting, drivers must also prove that they have completed at least three Motorsport UK sanctioned Bambino kart races, not just the Bambino time trial events. Alternatively, karters who have completed three Motorsport UK time trial events in the Bambino category, and are in the year of their eighth birthday, but have not yet reached their birthday, must also meet a minimum height of 125cm; however, under these circumstances drivers are restricted to a single venue for competition. Furthermore, for karters in this situation, progression to the Cadet category is also dependent on the driver completing an approved ARKS course, together with having their competition licence application endorsed by a recognised kart club (we will discuss kart clubs in the next section). The licence will then be held by said kart club, remaining valid for Cadet karting until the driver has reached their eighth birthday or gathered a Motorsport UK steward's signature on their upgrade card during at least three InterClub kart races. Following this process, and upon turning eight years old, karters can apply for an unrestricted InterClub Kart licence.

The main Cadet classes are:

➤ **The IAME Cadet class**, which uses 60cc unsealed two-stroke Parilla Gazelle engine.
➤ **The Honda Cadet class**, which uses a four-stroke Gx160 engine. The longevity of this engine makes this a very cost-effective option.

There are also Cadet class championships under the Motorsport UK British Kart Championships banner, discussed in the next section.

The next step is the Mini category, open to those aged between 11 and 14. A driver can enter the Mini classification upon turning 11, however once a karter has progressed to this or the subsequent category, they cannot revert back to Cadet karting, so make sure you are definitely ready to progress before making the commitment. Karters will need a National licence to be eligible for the Mini division. Upon reaching this stage, regulations start to become much stricter, with a minimum weight and height for the karter, along with a minimum class weight, all of which will be displayed in the specific class regulations.

Next up, we have the Junior category. Now things get very serious, and even more competitive. The Junior division is designed for karters who fall between the 13 to 16 years age bracket. Once again, a minimum driver weight must be adhered to; this is set out in the class regulations. Despite being eligible for the Junior category from the year of their 13th birthday, a karter is unable to contest gearbox karts until they actually hit their 13th birthday. Be aware that given the crossover of age range between the Mini and Junior categories, it is possible for some classes to span both divisions, providing all height and weight restrictions are met and the kart's performance is within the boundaries of the Mini category.

As a Mini or Junior karter, there are a number of classes you will be eligible to contest, such as:

➤ **Rotax Mini Max**
   The Rotax kart is one of the most popular karts in the sport. Despite being more expensive initially, the long life of the engines means they go a lot longer between engine rebuilds, balancing out or even reducing costs somewhat.
➤ **Junior Max**
   One of the most powerful junior classes, with a top speed of around 75mph.
➤ **Junior TKM** – A popular, more traditional kart.
➤ **Junior TKM four-stroke**
➤ **Junior TKM Extreme**
   This is a faster 115cc class for championships, however this is not used at some clubs.
➤ **Junior four-stroke classes**
   There are other four-stroke options for junior and senior categories, however they only operate at certain clubs.

Finally, we have the Senior category. Novice karters are eligible for the Senior category during the year in which they turn 16. Alternatively, karters who hold a Kart National A licence are eligible to compete in a Senior non-gearbox kart class from their 15th birthday. In similar fashion to preceding categories, a karter who has progressed to the senior discipline cannot revert back to the Mini or Junior division.

The most popular Senior classes to contest are the Rotax Max and X30, which also run as part of the British Kart Championships. However, there are a number of alternative options within your local club or circuit, as some classes only operate within certain localities. For example, the TKM Extreme class is very popular around the Midlands area.

Other classes eligible for those who are operating in the Senior category include the following:

➤ **TKM Extreme**
   Now popular with kart circuits in and around the Midlands area, the TKM Extreme class is aimed at drivers aged 16 and over. The engine creates 115cc. In order to manage costs, all chassis with new designs must be

registered and are only permitted every three years, ensuring a budget-friendly option. This class also now includes a Touch and Go start system (TAG).

➤ **Rotax Max**
This is the Senior equivalent of the Junior Max option. Karts within this class operate with a 125cc engine and TAG system. Like so many classes, bound by weight restrictions, drivers who exceed the set weight can enter the Rotax 177 class.

➤ **X30**
Manufactured by IAME, the X30 class is accepted by the majority of clubs and has its own British Championship under Motorsport UK regulations.

The final category is for gearbox karts. There is a Junior gearbox class that is open to 85cc karts, for drivers aged 13 to 17. Excluding this, gearbox karts offer much higher power and either have two pedals, a brake and accelerator, or three pedals, much like a car. As previously mentioned, gearbox karts tend to be raced at long circuit kart events.

Gearbox classes consist of the following:

➤ **KZ UK**
This is the most popular gearbox class. Although slightly more expensive in the first instance, karts within this class can lean towards being budget friendly in terms of running costs. Using a 125cc water cooled engine, the kart has a top speed of 90mph on a short circuit, and 110-120mph on a long circuit.

➤ **KZ1**
This is virtually the same as the kart mentioned above, although it is bound by more strict regulations.

➤ **Junior gearbox**
The Junior gearbox kart enjoys 85cc of engine prowess, from a Honda or TKM engine.

➤ **250 National**
The most powerful short circuit kart class, running with 250cc engines. Top speeds reach 100mph on short circuits and 140mph on long circuits. In comparison, twin cylinder Superkarts will reach around 170mph.

Away from professional competition, such as that sanctioned by Motorsport UK, the other option is indoor karting, aimed more at the casual kart racer; however, this can often be a good starting point for progressing into motorsport competition.

Championships and clubs
Championships

Those wanting to take up karting in a more professional manner will likely look to enter a championship. Many kart clubs around the UK will offer their own local or national championship competitions, however the most prestigious contests are those sanctioned by Motorsport UK – the British Kart Championships.

The British Kart Championships comprise a number of classes, each with its own championship status. Let's go through each of them to see what they include.

- **Rotax**

The Rotax Championship includes Mini Max, Junior Rotax, Senior Rotax and Rotax 177 classes. Since its inception, the reputation of the Rotax engine has grown over the years across the various categories and is easily one of the more popular options within the karting market.

After making its first appearance in 1997, the Rotax Max was revolutionary, with its self-starting procedure and centrifugal clutch. This concept immediately took off, with demand soon outweighing supply. Now used universally across all classes, karters can start using the Rotax engine from the age of seven, with various power outputs available depending on the respective classes.

Another popular feature of the Rotax Max is the warranty. Each engine can race in a competitive environment for a season before needing a rebuild; however, under the warranty each engine and rebuild components are covered. Given the durability of the engine, this means you are likely to find a good secondhand option on the market, which helps to make your journey as cost-effective as possible.

- **IAME**

Classes within the IAME championship consist of IAME Cadet, Mini X30, Junior X30 and Senior X30, with graduates of the IAME Cadet class progressing to the Mini X30 category, and so on.

The IAME Cadet category was first introduced as a class within the British Championships back in 2013. Upon advancing from IAME Cadet, a lot of young karters choose the heavily restricted X30 Mini. When the opportunity arises to graduate between the different IAME classes, there are a few fairly simple procedures that will make your kart eligible for that next step. For instance, for those who wish to switch from the X30 Mini to X30 Junior class, you just need to alter the restrictor size. Once you are ready to progress to the X30 Senior, simply remove the restrictor altogether and you're ready to go. Although a number of the X30 competitors will run under a team banner, there are still a large number of privateer entrants in this category; this again helps those who are budget conscious.

• **Honda Cadet**

The Honda Cadet is an ideal starting ground for young karters. With alumni including Tom Ingram, Lando Norris, George Russell and Alex Albon, it shows the level of talent that has come through the Honda Cadet ranks.

Utilising the Honda GX160 engine, this Cadet class is known for being very competitive, and, in turn, very popular with all manner of karters. A great way to learn your race craft, it connects that gap between budget-friendly club level racing and the route taken by those looking for a more professional path through the industry.

• **TKM**

Underneath the TKM championship banner sit the Junior TKM and TKM Extreme classes. In a bid to provide a competitive racing environment for karters, Formula TKM was born, and now with more than three decades of experience behind it, it is currently the UK's longest running class. With the likes of Jenson Button and Anthony Davidson as just some of its more well-known and successful graduates, TKM is a force to be reckoned with in the karting world.

With junior and senior classes available, drivers can navigate a successful route for themselves from the age of 11 and up, without the need to spend a fortune. Championships such as the TKM division is proof that success can be discovered on a lower budget, you don't need to spend millions of pounds. Just remember that many championships, regardless of discipline, are keen to keep costs to a minimum. The more budget friendly a championship is, the more drivers it will attract. Restrictions put in place in the karting ranks, such as sealed engines, all help to ensure a level playing field. The TKM championship is no different: strict methods such as controlled tyre options and engine tuning restrictions ensure the karts remain as equal as possible.

• **KZ2**

One of the gearbox classes, KZ2 is the fastest class within the short circuit British Championship stable, reaching 90mph at some venues. Popular across Europe, renowned graduates of the KZ2 class include none other than Max Verstappen.

The KZ2 is a notch above other classes, with 30 gear changes each lap and 0-60mph in less than three seconds, it is extremely physically demanding on the driver. A larger outlay initially than some of the other Junior and Senior karts, the KZ2 can still be a cost-effective vehicle to manage on a long-term basis.

- **Bambino**

The Bambino class was created to give youngsters the opportunity to experience karting first-hand. As discussed under the Bambino category, the Bambino class is still in its infancy, however since 2018 those karters who are aged seven and contesting the Bambino category are able to compete at a Motorsport UK championship competition level.

Clubs

I mentioned earlier in this chapter that there are upwards of 150 kart circuits in the UK, many of these will operate their own clubs and organise competitions at a specific venue, but there are so many other, stand-alone clubs as well, that will race at various circuits across the country. A good starting point is to contact your local kart club. During this section I will discuss many of the karting clubs throughout the UK in more detail, also noting which circuit(s) they usually use. The clubs mentioned here are all registered with the Association of British Kart Clubs, and also affiliated with Motorsport UK.

- **Bayford Meadow**

Located in Sittingbourne, Kent, Bayford Meadow holds a race day every fourth Sunday. Dubbed the home of club racing in Kent, Bayford Meadow has been organising Motorsport UK sanctioned kart events for over 20 years. The venue also plays host to the Kent Kart Championship.

- **British Historic Kart Club**

The British Historic Kart Club (BHKC) was formed in 2005. The club operates at various circuits, from track days, to race meetings and demonstrations at events such as the Donington Historic Festival.

- **Camberley Kart Club**

Utilising Blackbushe Airfield in Surrey, race day for Camberley Kart Club is the fourth Saturday in the month. Although it is a fairly short circuit, it poses a great technical challenge to drivers.

- **Chasewater Kart Club**

After using a venue at Chasewater, Staffordshire for events for many years, the club is currently looking for a new venue. More details regarding Chasewater Kart Club can be found online.

- **Clay Pigeon Kart Club**

Clay Pigeon is one of the more well-known venues in the karting world. Based in Dorset, it plays host to many local and national karting championship events. Race day is the second Sunday in the month.

• **Cheshire Kart Racing Club**
Using the Hooton Park circuit, the Cheshire Kart Racing Club is based near Ellesmere Port. The circuit was built in 2006 on the site of the former Hooton Airfield. A dedicated karting circuit, the venue follows the approved standard as set by Motorsport UK.

• **Club 100 Kart Club**
Club 100 is described as the fastest arrive-and-drive championship in the UK. The Club is based in Kent, however events take place at a number of different kart circuits across the country. The main areas of competition include Endurance, Sprint, SP60, The Club 100 Experience and Young Driver's Championship. Each area includes multiple championship options across a number of rounds throughout the season. Club 100 was designed for karters who have sampled indoor and outdoor four-stroke rental karting, who would like to progress to a more competitive point. To contest Club 100 events, you will need a K-X licence, however you do not need to purchase the Motorsport UK Go Karting pack or pass an ARKS test in order to get this. Acting as an arrive-and-drive championship, this is the perfect in between step for karters looking to become more serious, before making the commitment to buy a kart and enter a Motorsport UK race event. Exclusive test days are available for those looking to join Club 100.

• **Cumbria Kart Club**
Cumbria Kart Club uses the Rowrah circuit, just a few miles from Frizington in Cumberland. Race days take place on the second Sunday of each month.

• **East of Scotland Kart Club**
Race days under the East of Scotland Kart Club take place on various days near the village of Crail in Fife. With four different circuit layouts available, the venue has plenty to offer its members. Club championship races with the Club cost £40, making it one of the best value karting venues in the country.

• **Forest Edge Kart Club**
Barton Stacey near Andover is the venue of choice for Forest Edge Kart Club, with race days taking place during the first Sunday of the month.

• **Dragon Kart Club**
Based in Wales, Glan-y-Gors Park near Conwy plays host to Dragon Kart Club events. Race days at the venue take place on the second Sunday of the month.

- **FP4K Kart Club**

The FP4K Kart Club takes its members to the best kart circuits the South of England has to offer. Venues include Mansell Raceway, Clay Pigeon, Lydd International, Camberley Kart Club, Bayford Meadow, Rissington and Thruxton. Race days vary throughout the season, with the Club's calendar spanning April to November.

- **F100 Kart Club**

This is a kart club with a difference. It is a national kart racing series, focusing on karts from the 1990s. Karts are raced in the same condition as they would have been presented during that decade.

- **Grampian Kart Club**

Another club located in Scotland, the Grampian Kart Club organises races at Boyndie, near Banff. Race meetings take place during the second Sunday of the month, between March and October.

- **Hunts Kart Club/Kimbolton**

The Hunts Kart Club operates on the second Sunday of the month, at the Kimbolton kart circuit, just 10 miles from Huntingdon.

- **Jersey Kart and Motor Club**

The Jersey Kart and Motor Club organises events on various days throughout the season, at the dedicated venue at Sorel Point, St John in Jersey.

- **Fulbeck Kart Club (previously Lincs Kart Club)**

Making use of the Fulbeck circuit in Lincolnshire, Fulbeck Kart Club's race meetings take place during the fourth Sunday on the month. As well as test days, the club hosts a number of Motorsport UK championship race meetings between February and November, at the Fulbeck circuit.

- **Lydd International Kart Club**

Lydd International generally hosts race meetings on the second Sunday of the month, at the Lydd International circuit in Kent.

- **Manchester and Buxton Kart Club**

Dubbed the North's premier kart racing club, the Manchester and Buxton Kart Club events take place at Glan-y-Gors Park near Conwy. Race meetings tend to occur during the fourth Sunday of the month.

- **Mansell Kart Racing Club**
Based near Honiton in Devon, the Mansell Kart Racing Club has more than 50 years of expertise behind it. Operating from Mansell Raceway, formerly Dunkeswell Airfield, the Club offers multiple events throughout the year, each set to a Motorsport UK standard. Events tend to take place on the last Sunday of the month.

- **NATSKA (National Schools Karting Association)**
The National Schools Karting Association operates at various kart circuits throughout the UK, with events taking place between April and October.

- **North of Scotland Kart Club**
The North of Scotland Kart Club operates on either the fourth or last Sunday of the month. Race meetings take place in the Scottish Highlands, at Golspie in Sutherland.

- **RAF Motor Sports Association (Kart Section)**
Operating at various circuits, this is the karting division of the RAF motorsport team.

- **Rissington Kart Club**
Based at Little Rissington RAF Station, Rissington Kart Club hosts all manner of karting championship events, usually operating on the first Sunday of the month.

- **Shenington Kart Club**
Based in the heart of motorsport country, near Banbury, Shenington Kart Club hosts a wide variety of events, including Motorsport UK British Kart Championship race meetings. Events generally take place on the third Sunday of the month.

- **South Yorkshire Kart Club**
Based at Wombwell Sports Stadium near Barnsley, the South Yorkshire Kart Club events take place on the second Sunday of the month.

- **Trent Valley Kart Club**
Another Lincolnshire-based club, Trent Valley uses the specialist karting circuit, PF International (PFI) for its events. With race meetings generally taking place on the first Sunday of the month, Trent Valley hosts an abundance of events, including Motorsport UK British Kart Championship race meetings.

- **Ulster Kart Club**

Representing Northern Ireland, the Ulster Kart Club operates on various Sundays throughout the season. Hosting its events, Nutts Corner is a purpose-built facility.

- **Warden Law Kart Club**

Warden Law Kart Club uses the Warden Law Motorsports Centre in Sunderland for all of its track activities. Race meeting dates vary, with Sundays typically the race day for the Club.

- **West of Scotland Kart Club**

Generally operating race meetings during the third Sunday of the month, the West of Scotland Kart Club is based at Larkhall Circuit. Built in 1961, the circuit has been developed over the years, and now features a state-of-the-art facility.

- **Whilton Mill Kart Club**

Based near Daventry, Whilton Mill Kart Club holds race meetings on the fourth Sunday of the month. As well as karting, Whilton Mill caters for a variety of outdoor activities.

There are other clubs not featured on this list that will operate under their own organisation. One such club is the Bambino Kart Club. The Bambino Kart Club (BKC) organises its own competition, the BKC Series. Founded in 2011, it is now the most prominent and successful Bambino karting championship in the UK. In recent years, the Club has also progressed to other classes, welcoming Cadet and Junior karters into its competitive ranks as well.

Classes currently supported in the Bambino Kart Club include:

➤ Comer C50 Bambino
➤ Mighte Bambino
➤ IAME M1 Bambino
➤ Honda Cadet
➤ IAME Cadet
➤ OK Junior

Each event takes place over two days, with practice, qualifying and heats on the Saturday, followed by further heats and the finals on the Sunday. Many of the circuits discussed in the Clubs section feature on the Bambino Kart Club calendar, with venues such as Whilton Mill, Fulbeck and Rowrah all included.

With a large emphasis on guiding young karters through the early stages of their motorsport career, the Bambino Kart Club likes to ensure its members have fun and learn the skills of racing in a safe environment.

As well as the various clubs operating their own championships and events, there are a number of other opportunities to enter into the world of competitive karting, whether it's on a more informal or professional level.

Thruxton Circuit, based near Andover, Hampshire, is one of many arrive-and-drive karting circuits in the UK. As well as the fast-paced race circuit, the venue also has its own kart centre. With three different layouts available, including the national, club and full circuits, there is a good variety of challenges. In terms of competitions, there is something to suit all abilities, with the venue catering for everyone from absolute novice karters to those who are more experienced.

In terms of the karts available, Thruxton Kart Centre has cadet karts for drivers aged eight years and over, karts for junior drivers who are aged 12 years and over, and adult karts for those aged 15 years and over. The venue offers arrive-and-drive competition, as well as Grand Prix and Super Prix events.

Another popular venue amongst the karting fraternity is Daytona Karting. A prominent company in the world of kart circuits, Daytona Karting offers premier outdoor karting experiences for all levels and abilities. With a few branches in the UK, including Milton Keynes, Surrey and Tamworth, the circuits are fairly central and accessible for a lot of drivers.

Daytona Karting can be a strong starting point for karters looking for a more focused career as a racing driver. All racing equipment is provided, negating the need to own and run your own kart, and helping a great deal with budget restraints. There are plenty of different events to choose from, from full championships to special one-off competitions, private and corporate events.

In terms of championships, Daytona run a number of competitions at its various sites, each aimed at different age groups and skill levels. Karters who have graduated from Daytona Karting championships have gone on to bigger and better accomplishments, including the likes of Sam Bird. Following his karting successes, Sam has since gone on to compete in a number of high-profile championships, from single-seaters to sportscars and is now a successful FIA Formula E racer. The Daytona Karting championships include the following:

> Junior InKart Championship
> Aimed at drivers from the age of eight years old. The InKart Championship includes different age and weight categories to ensure a level of equality between drivers. This is one of a number of suitable starting points for those looking to start their karting career. Races take place at all Daytona Karting venues, with races for Cadet, Junior and Senior class competitors available.

> Adult InKart Championship
> With a number of karts available, the Adult Championship caters for those aged 14 years and over. Drivers over the age of 14 can compete in the

SODI karts, whereas those aged 16 years and over can contest the DMAX karts. Drivers who are more experienced but still only 14 or 15 years old can compete in the DMAX classes with the correct approval beforehand. To progress from the junior to senior ranks of competition, drivers must have graduated from the Daytona Karting Race School.

➤ **D60 Champs**
Specific to the Daytona Karting Sandown Park circuit, the D60 Champs is an hour-long Iron Man style competition. The event includes practice and qualifying sessions, followed by a 60-minute endurance race.

➤ **Summer and Winter Championships**
Daytona Karting also runs separate summer and winter championship events that run on the first Sunday of each month. Summer championships run between April and September, with the winter event taking place between October and March. Drivers are separated into light and heavyweight classes, with trophies awarded within each class.

In addition to the above championships, Daytona Karting offers various other arrive-and-drive packages. Starting with Bambino and Junior level karters, packages can cater for those looking to gain some experience, as well as more informal events. The Daytona Race School is an ideal starting point for younger karters looking to progress through the ranks on a competitive level. Those in the Bambino category (six to seven years old) have a number of training modules available to them at the Daytona venues, as they get to grips with their first karts. From here, Bambino drivers can graduate to the arrive-and-drive packages. As previously mentioned, karters between the ages of eight and 15 are categorised in a junior position. The Daytona Race School is very friendly with younger drivers. Working around schooling and other commitments, the programme takes place during school holidays. Once a driver graduates from the Daytona Race School they are then eligible to progress to the InKart Championships as a fully fledged member.

Live timing is available for races at each of the Daytona Karting venues, allowing drivers to track their progress from race to race, as well as against their fellow competitors.

Another popular venue is Raceway Kart Centre in Lincolnshire. With competitions for karters of all ages, from six-year-olds through to senior competitors, there is something to suit everyone. For those looking to start at the very beginning, Raceway Kart Centre hosts a Bambino Exclusive Training School, to help those who are brand new to the world of karting. From important information about safety to detailed tuition on-circuit, this programme is a suitable first step for young karters. With one-to-one coaching, the Bambino Training School includes six steps:

> Step One – Safety briefing and suit up
> Step Two – Track walk with the most experienced members of the team
> Step Three – A look around the kart and its controls
> Step Four – Track session. An instructor will lead the way in a separate kart to demonstrate the way around the circuit
> Step Five – A break and a session working through the map of the circuit
> Step Six – Another track session with or without an instructor, depending on your skill level

Once you have successfully completed these six steps, you will receive Raceway Kart Centre membership, a medal, and a certificate to prove you are qualified. Following the completion of this training course, you can book further exclusive practice sessions and lessons at the centre, to further enhance your track performance. Additional practice sessions will cost £15 for 10 minutes, or £20 for 15 minutes, with individual lessons for £60 each. This is an ideal situation to practise, enhance and develop your race skills. It is along the lines of a track day equivalent that you would normally do as a method of car racing preparation.

Many clubs and circuits will offer this type of service, which is essentially a track day for karters. Whichever circuit or club you decide to book, with professional tuition on hand throughout the day or session, it is the ideal opportunity to help prepare you for your first, and even subsequent races.

Another popular venue for kart races is Buckmore Park. Hosting a range of fun and competitive events, Buckmore Park has established itself as a proving ground for up-and-coming karting talent. Based in Kent, Buckmore Park is an outdoor karting venue, approved by Motorsport UK. Having been formally owned by World Champion on two and four wheels, John Surtees, it shows the quality of the track. Situated close to London, Buckmore Park is considered Britain's busiest circuit.

With its own racing school, the venue has been preparing drivers for a successful career in motorsport since 1972 and is still a prominent part of the karting community today. The main racing school caters for karters aged eight and over, with a separate Bambino School for karters aged six to seven years old. Teaching methods range between introductory courses, to more in-depth programmes.

In terms of racing, Buckmore Park hosts a number of popular events, from its Hire Kart Club, offering shorter sprint style races to slightly longer endurance and team events. Given its rich heritage, Buckmore Park is usually one of the go-to circuits when it comes to competitive karting.

Progressing from karting
Upon reaching the ripe old age of 16 or 17 years old, the time comes to think

of the next step in your motor racing career. There are plenty of indoor karting facilities across the country, if you would like to maintain your competitive edge in a kart, however for those looking into the more professional motorsport route, the natural progression is to move into car racing.

At this point there are countless opportunities available for those stepping into car racing. You may have had a route in mind from the early stages of your karting exploits, for instance some people opt for the single-seater route, whereas others prefer the tin tops path. One main thing to remember, do not be disheartened if you deviate from your planned route. There are a great deal of factors that can contribute to this, from budget restraints to unexpected opportunities that are just too good to turn down. I know of so many racing drivers who were destined for the single-seater route, with Formula One as their ultimate goal, however a slight, unexpected deviation into tin tops led them down the GT route instead, and yet they still flourished.

During the next section I will go through what's available in the world of car racing. As I mentioned, you may already have a route mapped out, but it's nice to have a few options, or to know what else is available.

CAR RACING
The car

So, you're ready to start car racing. Whether you are making the natural progression from karting, or you are a complete novice, making the leap into car racing is very exciting. It goes without saying that the car is a vital piece of equipment, but the type of car you choose depends on the discipline, championship or series you are planning to contest. There are a great deal of options available, from single-seaters to tin tops. Those drivers who have a number of years karting under their belt will often plan for the single-seater route, with a goal of one day reaching the realms of Formula One. However, there are those drivers whose dream is perhaps more endurance based, and so the tin top and GT route is more for them. For those who are complete novices, working to a specific budget and looking at standard UK club racing, you may find the tin top route more appealing.

When deciding which car to choose, some people opt to transform a road car into a race car, perhaps a road car that has been sat idle on the driveway for too long, whereas others may choose to purchase a ready-to-race car that requires very little work. This decision is purely personal preference, but it also depends on your own mechanical ability, the amount of spare time you have to dedicate to such a project, and, of course, your budget.

As mentioned briefly at the beginning of this section, one of the first points to consider is which discipline you are planning to contest – for instance hillclimb, sprinting or circuit racing? Once you have determined this, and whether you would prefer to race a single-seater, a tin top or other type of road car, your choice of car will start to become that bit clearer.

Hillclimbing and sprinting events comprise multiple classes, including some road car classes, meaning you don't have to worry about modifying your daily runaround into a high-powered, turbo-charged race car. You can arrive in your daily runner, post your competitive runs, then head home again, all in the same car, and hopefully with a trophy strapped into your passenger seat. Classes are not just restricted to road cars, however: events and championships are made up of different categories, with cars grouped together based on power, or type of car, for instance. Hillclimb events take place at hillclimb-specific venues throughout the UK. Each venue will hold its own events on a regular basis; for instance Harewood Speed Hillclimb in Yorkshire will host a number of rounds throughout the season for the various classes. Competitors may choose to compete locally and only enter events at their local venue, where they are a member, or may prefer to sample some other hillclimb venues for a bit of variety. There is also the British Hillclimb Championship, slightly more serious and extremely competitive, and which travels around the country. Sprinting, on the other hand, takes place at various venues, including race circuits, and is a timed event, operating in a similar way to a hillclimb.

Circuit racing requires a somewhat different approach to hillclimbing or sprinting, for most championships and series at least. We will come to this in more detail throughout this section.

As I alluded to earlier, it is always worth having an idea of not only which discipline, but also the specific championship or series you're aiming for, particularly if you are building your car. Each championship or series enforces a set of strict regulations that each driver must adhere to, to ensure that each car matches the eligibility criteria. However, you will also need to refer to the Blue Book to make sure your car is fitted with the appropriate safety equipment, such as the correct seatbelts, roll-over protection system, and fire extinguisher.

You may remember I mentioned essential stickers whilst discussing where to buy race equipment. Although stickers may seem insignificant, they are rather important from a scrutineering point of view. Regardless of what type of race car you have chosen, you will need to display a certain batch of stickers in specific places on your car. First of all, as a novice driver, you will need to display a novice cross, which is a yellow square with a black cross on it. This is to let other drivers know that you are indeed a novice and new to the circuit. Don't worry, you won't be stuck with this forever, but need to keep it on your car until you have completed six races. Once you have collected the first six signatures on your upgrade card (as discussed in Chapter 1), you can proudly remove your novice cross. Other stickers you need to display include 'Tow' with an arrow pointing towards your car's tow point. This is to assist the circuit recovery team, should you need them to help at all. It helps to speed up recovery time, and also saves unnecessary damage to your race car. You must also display a thunderbolt symbol to let the trackside marshals know where your electrical cut off switch is, and the letter E next to your extinguisher. In the event of an emergency it helps officials to know which nozzles to pull to either set off the extinguisher or cut the electrics.

Once you have a rough idea of the championship you plan to contest, make yourself familiar with the supplementary regulations set out by the organising club or championship. Make the championship regulations and the Motorsport UK Blue Book your bedtime reading. Once you know them both inside out, you can't go wrong. If you're struggling with the regulations, you can always clarify any queries with your organising club, who will be more than happy to help. Asking in advance what you may think is an obvious question is much better than being caught out during a race meeting.

Those championships and series with multiple classes will have different regulations per class, so make sure you know which regulations you are working with. The specifications for each class will differ from one another, so clarify which class your car is eligible for beforehand. If you are preparing your car to race next season, keep a weather eye on the championship information, as regulations can change from one season to the next. Some of this advice may seem basic, but for those who are brand new to motorsport, there is an awful lot to digest. Some of the regulations to be aware of are:

> Tyres – the type of tyre allowed, and if there are any restrictions to the number of tyres you can use throughout a single season. The number of tyres isn't usually an issue in the early realms of club racing, but it is always something to be aware of. For the most part, with tin tops and race versions of road cars, the type of tyre falls into the 1A, 1B or 1C category. All championships and series will work together with a specific tyre supplier, and so drivers are only permitted to use tyres from the named supplier. This will pointed out in the championship regulations.

> Weight – the minimum weight of the car and driver, both together and separately.

> Power to weight ratio – this will determine which class you are eligible for in a multi-class championship or series.

> Power output of your race car – engine capacity, brake horsepower (bhp) and the power at the flywheel may all be taken into consideration.

In some cases, you may be required to take your car to a rolling road, to clarify the engine output, amongst other details. This can sometimes be arranged as a personal preference, particularly if your car is secondhand, just to clarify how powerful your engine is. However, it may be a compulsory requirement of the championship to ensure a level playing field. In the case of it being a compulsory measure, some championships may dictate which rolling road you are allowed to use, as some will be approved over others, however there is usually a selection to choose from, depending on which one is closest to you.

Looking at the technical regulations for your car more closely, you are not permitted to make any modifications that aren't permitted by your championship or series. It is important to follow the set regulations to the letter. The regulations I will discuss below apply to all drivers, whether you build your own car or not, it is vital you make sure certain aspects are correct, even down to your seat and harness.

When it comes to your engine, suspension, brakes, cooling system, wheels, and tyres, the Motorsport UK Blue Book has detailed a set of standard regulations that must be adhered to. There will then be a set of more precise supplementary regulations to follow, as defined for your specific championship or series, so it is always worth double checking both. The two will work hand in hand, rather than contradict one another.

In terms of seating, it is pretty self-explanatory, but your seat must fit you securely, and be firmly fastened to your car. Seats will differ between different cars, for instance the Blue Book states that seats within a single-seater race car must allow the driver to climb in or escape within five seconds. When it comes to regulations, you will see the word homologation mentioned a great deal, particularly as you move up the motorsport ladder. Homologation is the granting of approval by an official authority. Many equipment items within motorsport, regardless of whether it is at club level or international, will be homologated. This includes seats and seatbelts, however it is only for FIA governed events, rather than a general club level motor race. Anything that is homologated with have an expiration date. If your seat and harness have a homologation number on them, you will need to take note of the expiration date. In the case of your harness this is usually five years. If you are building a race car, it has also been advised that the seat is one of the final items to buy, because if it takes you a few years to build your car, your seat may have expired before you can race, meaning you will have to buy a new seat that is in date.

Some types of cars may have a different kind of seat altogether, for example in the case of Caterham racing there is the option to have a bead seat moulded to your personal shape and comfort. You can buy the bead seat resin kit to make yourself at home from a vendor such as Demon Tweeks, or you can have one professionally made by a company like Indi Seat or Schroth. To purchase a kit from Demon Tweeks, prices start at £143.66 (inclusive of VAT), and increase depending on the size of the kit you want to buy. Seat kits are available in 15, 30,

40, 50, 70, 90 or 110-litre options. The larger the kit, the larger the seat will be. Once you have your bead seat, it will need covering in a fire-resistant material, such as fireproof gaffer tape, in order to comply with new regulations. This will then ensure your seat passes any scrutineering checks.

Although you will come across different brands of seatbelts in different cars, the mechanism is largely the same. You will find the most common style of seatbelt used in many motorsport disciplines is a six-point harness. The harness fastens with a quick release mechanism on your front as a safety feature, enabling you to exit the car in seconds if you need to. The harness is referred to as 'six-point' due to the fact it is bolted to the car by six points, two either side of the driver, two to the rear of the seat and two between the legs. The straps fasten in a similar way, a strap over each shoulder, a strap across the lap and two straps between the legs, which all come together in a clasp. When the harness is fastened, the straps must be pulled as tight as possible. This may feel strange at first, but they basically need to pin you in your seat. If you can still slide or move about in your seat, they are not tight enough. When fastened, the clasp should sit against your stomach. Some people, once they have pulled their shoulder straps tight, leave the clasp sat higher up against their rib cage. Do not do this: if you have an incident or a sudden stop it could damage or break your ribs. Always position it lower down. The quick release clasp means you can unfasten yourself and exit your car in seconds: to operate this you simply twist the fastening and all straps will unclip straight away.

For those championships that state a minimum weight, you will need to ensure you meet this when required. There will be a set weight for your car, however your car will often be weighed with you in it after a race, so you need to know what this full weight equates to. The minimum weight dictated in your championship regulations will be the weight of your car as it crosses the finish line, minus you. Some championships may include your weight with the weight of the car as an overall total. Before your car goes out on-circuit for a race, you must be confident that it will hit the minimum weight when you finish the race. For this you will need to take into consideration the amount of fuel you put into the car, you don't want to risk running out on-circuit, but the amount of fuel you have left in your car at the end will add to the overall weight. Another element to factor in, is if your car should lose any bodywork during the race. In the case of a tin top this could be a wing mirror, or, in the case of a Caterham, this could be, and most likely will be, a front or rear wing.

If your car is underweight, perhaps because you are a lighter driver, you will have to insert ballast into your car. If you need to do so, the ballast must be attached to the shell or chassis with four bolts. The bolts used to do this must have a minimum diameter of 8mm each. The precise nature of this requirement indicates just how important it is to abide by the regulations and ensure your car and equipment is up to scratch.

One final cost associated with your race car is insurance. Upon signing on for a race meeting, you are covered to some degree, however this does not apply to your race car when on-circuit. The decision of whether to insure your race car or not is a personal preference. I know many people who do not opt for cover, and some that do. It is more than likely something you will never need, but it's up to you whether you want to risk it on the off chance you do need some insurance cover. Again, this is all budget dependent. Your race club may often have a partnership with a motorsport insurer, offering a discount as part of your membership benefits. If not, there are a number of insurers who operate within the motorsport industry, such as REIS, Ryan Motorsport and Adrian Flux, all of whom have been involved in the sport for many years. It is always worth contacting them for a quote when setting your budget, to see what's available. You may even receive a discount either through your membership club benefits or with your race licence. When it comes to renewing your race licence, there are also a number of benefits through Motorsport UK, including enhanced personal accident insurance when competing with Bluefin Sport, 15% discount on competition car insurance with REIS, and 15% discount on road car insurance with Adrian Flux, as well as discounts from Halfords and cash back on tyres, so it is worth investigating all avenues to see what's available.

Where to find your race car
So, you've decided which discipline and championship or series you wish to contest, now for the car. If your championship of choice is a one-make competition your choice has already been made for you, making it slightly easier. However, for those planning to enter multi-class racing, or racing that features different cars, it is slightly more convoluted. In this instance, once you find a car you like, a bit of research goes a long way. Have a look through previous races to get an idea of the popularity and competitiveness of different cars, you may find that the majority of drivers tend to run the same make and model of car in multi-class racing, based on how competitive it is. For instance, you will see a number of Honda Civic Type R race cars in the Hot Hatch Championship in Class A, due to it proving to be a successful and competitive entity. However, remember that as useful as this is, the individual driver has a lot to do with the performance of the car, so try not to read too much into lap times. As mentioned in the karting section earlier in this chapter, there are a number of external factors that contribute to the success rate of a car, from the driver to mechanical issues, or even the set-up on the car. I have known drivers turn down a perfectly good car due to previous results showing it finishing at the back of the grid. However, in the hands of a new owner the same car will finish on the podium. Although I

wouldn't recommend basing your final decision solely on this element, it is a good way to gauge which cars are the more popular choice when purchasing your first race car.

As with purchasing a road car, there are many outlets to browse when searching for your race car. Always consider the points mentioned above, and remember to bear in mind the class you are entering for multi-class championships.

One of the most popular websites to search for your car, and a good starting point, is Race Cars Direct. As mentioned earlier, Race Cars Direct is a popular central hub, used by motorsport buyers and sellers alike. It's the eBay of the motorsport world if you like. It is usually one of the first stops for those buying or selling anything transport related within the motorsport industry, from race cars to trailers, and a good place to start looking if you plan to transport the car yourself. Self-transport is another thing to consider, and something to factor into your budget, but this is something we will come to later in this chapter.

Social media is another useful source, and it is certainly worthwhile making use of this. I will discuss more about the importance of social media and how to use it correctly in Chapter 6, but for now let's focus on finding your race car. Championship-specific groups and pages are usually well populated with cars and equipment for sale, as well as tips and advice from your fellow competitors, so it is always worth joining these groups if you can. General automotive or marque-specific groups and pages are also worth joining, such as a Ford Fiesta group, especially for those planning to transform a road car into a race car, as you will often find a relatively cheap car for sale that you can transform into a successful racer. Alternatively, have a look at the championship organiser's website. For instance, the 750 Motor Club has a classified ads section on the club website, as does the Caterham Graduates Racing Club; these are always worth a browse. In this case, the 750 Motor Club runs a vast number of championships and series', which come with a wide variety of cars, whereas the cars for sale with the Caterham Graduates Racing Club will be more restricted – as the name suggests it is a Caterham series.

You may also find that race teams in the championship you're interested in, or similar championships, have cars for sale, so it is worth speaking to people in the know to widen your search parameters as much as possible. Another avenue to try is eBay, particularly if you are planning to build or develop a car yourself, this could be a worthwhile exercise, leading you to something very cost effective indeed. Always remember that wherever you purchase your car from, there many be an option to also collect some spare parts at the same time. The seller may also include spare wheels and tyres or parts that they no longer need if they are not keeping the car, which will of course work in your favour.

The trailer

You have found and purchased your race car, but now you need some way of transporting it to race meetings, and somewhere safe to store it. Firstly, I will go through the various options for self-transporting your race car, and then look at storage options.

If you have decided to transport your race car yourself, as the majority of people tend to do, you will need to factor in the costs of a trailer. Trailers vary a great deal, in terms of the type of trailer, size and weight. The race car you have will also determine which sort of trailer you opt for, because it has to fit comfortably. It goes without saying that you will also need to make sure you have an appropriate tow vehicle, of course.

If you choose the tin top route, you will need a trailer to reflect this, as it will need to cater for the car's size and weight. When considering the type of trailer you could opt for an open trailer or a covered trailer. Open trailers are basically just that, something to simply load your car onto to transport it, whereas covered trailers come in a range of styles and sizes – this is where it could become rather expensive. Some more basic covered trailers have space for your car and that's it, whereas others have space for a spare set of tyres, fuel cans and a toolbox, as well as your car. A covered trailer also becomes beneficial when you are set up in the paddock, as it gives you a base, somewhere to set up your kettle (another essential piece of equipment), store your belongings safely, and shelter if the weather becomes unpleasant.

Some uncovered trailers have storage boxes attached to them, which can be used for fuel cans, for instance. They often come with a tyre rack, to make transporting your spare set of wheels that bit easier. When it comes to looking at trailers, one of the things that will also help you decide will be your tow vehicle. If you have a van, you will likely be able to transport all or most of your equipment in there safely, so you don't need to allow for a more elaborate trailer. However if your tow car is the family estate car, not only will you be limited on space, but you may also not want the smell of fuel seeping through from the fuel cans in the back, so you will need to think about a trailer with an appropriate storage facility for your equipment. Buying a trailer seems simple, but these are all things to take into consideration, that you may not have thought of.

If a covered trailer is more to your liking, and you have the budget for it, there are then different types of cover to choose from. You can either opt for the canopy style cover, or a solid clam cover; again, this depends largely on your budget and personal preference. The main names in the trailer business are Brian James, PRG and Eco-Trailer, and you will often see these around the paddock.

In addition to buying your trailer, whether it is covered or uncovered, you will also need to ensure you have ratchet straps, to secure the car during transport.

It may seem obvious, but ensure you have enough ratchet straps to strap down each corner of the car. Although buying less straps may save you a bit of money, if your car is not secure it could be more expensive in the long run. In the case of open top cars, such as single-seaters and Caterhams, you will also need a car cover. The last thing you want is a pool of water on your driving seat as you're about to climb in. In terms of maintenance, don't forget, as with your road car, your trailer may also need to be serviced every so often, to ensure it is fit for purpose. It is highly recommended you have your trailer serviced, to ensure its brakes, for instance, are still fully functioning.

Another consideration is the type of ramps the trailer has. Some extend with a little pull whilst still attached to the trailer, making them easy to use, whereas others will need to be lifted from their storage position and attached to the back of the trailer for loading. Either way they are usually fairly light, but take this into consideration before purchasing your trailer, especially if you are likely to be loading the car alone. It makes your job so much easier.

Storing your car and trailer

One of the biggest hurdles to overcome is where to store your race car and trailer if you are transporting your own car. This shouldn't be an issue that discourages you from racing, as it can be easily solved. It largely depends on your budget.

Finding a transport and storage solution as early as possible will be a big item to cross off your to-do list. If you have a spacious driveway to park your trailer and a garage for your race car, this is perfect, but don't worry if you don't, there are other options available – you don't need to frantically move to a new house. First of all, for those who will be storing and transporting your race car yourself, there are always storage facilities available, whether that's for your race car or trailer, or both. You may even be located close to a motorsport team who will happily store your trailer for you. Of course, things like this may incur an additional cost, but it's cheaper than moving house, put it that way. Again, this all depends on your budget.

If you do transport your race car yourself, don't forget to factor in a cost for your towing licence. If you are of a certain age, this may not be an issue for you, as 'grandfather rights' will entitle you to tow your race car and trailer legally. You may even be lucky enough to have a parent or friend who will accompany you to race meetings, who would be willing and able to tow the car for you.

Depending on the championship or series you sign up to, there may be teams that offer transport, race preparation, and race weekend mechanical support, ideal for those who are not very mechanically minded, or perhaps don't have the space to store a race car and trailer. The ability to store and transport your own car and equipment will help those who are on a tighter budget, but it is certainly worth knowing all of your options and weighing up which is best for you.

With the mention of race teams, this brings me to another useful point worth investigating: the option of race team support. Even at club level, this is a valuable option for some drivers, it's not just for the British Touring Car Championship and British GT Championship. For those drivers who are not very mechanically minded, or perhaps those who have limited time between work and race weekends to tinker with your race car, finding a race team to help you along the way can be mightily beneficial. This may be something you consider more when you have enjoyed a few seasons of racing, rather than your first season, but as I keep saying, it's all very budget dependent.

Having a race team on board can be extremely useful, especially as a novice. You will find professional race teams in all manner of race paddocks, all of whom will offer a varying level of support. For example, if you still like to have the option to look after your own race car at home, but don't have the facility to transport it yourself, a team may offer you a transport package. You will find options range from storage and transport to emergency race weekend support and full race weekend support. The difference between the support packages being that emergency race weekend support means you look after yourself unless you need severe mechanical assistance, whereas with full support, you have the luxury of turning up to a race weekend to see your race car sat waiting for you under your team's awning, prepped, washed and ready to go, and the only thing you need to do all weekend is jump in the car and race, the team does the rest. This also negates having to buy extra equipment, such as extra tools and pit equipment. Again, as expected, there are associated costs with each of these options that differ from championship to championship and team to team. Even the same paddock can present vast differences in the cost of team support.

If you like the sound of team support but you don't have a race team in your locality, don't worry. If a team is looking after your car, you only need to concentrate on getting yourself to the race meetings. As an example, CTS Motorsport is an experienced and highly qualified, multi-championship winning race team based in North Lincolnshire. The team currently operates in a variety of Caterham paddocks, such as the Caterham Graduates Racing Club and Toyo Tires 7 Race Series, as well as the Ginetta paddock, alongside the British Touring Car and British GT Championships. The majority of the team's drivers are not local, they tend to live all over the UK and even in Hong Kong. A race team is not like a regular garage, you're not usually just popping in on a whim. Any work your car needs following your last track session will be carried out ready for your next outing, so don't let location deter you from using a team if that option works for you.

Other essential equipment

Now you have your race car and trailer, but what else counts as an essential item for race meetings or track days? I will go through a list of items in this section, some of which will be very obvious, however if you have never been in a race paddock setting before, in a competitive sense at least, you may not have thought of some of them. There is also an essential items check list in Appendix 2, which includes your admin essentials as well as tools and your race kit, for you to use before each event, helping make your preparation that bit easier.

One useful piece of equipment is a pop-up awning. This can be very useful in an open paddock space. Depending on the championship or series you enter, you may be allocated pit garages for your race weekend, or you may be allocated a spot in the main paddock. This will also depend on which club you compete with. For example, if you compete with MSVR and your championship or series runs alongside the GT Cup package, you won't be allocated garages, as the GT Cup will be given garage space, being the biggest and most high-profile championship in attendance that weekend. Some cars are allocated garage space due to the prominent stature of the championship, whereas some require a more protected space due to the car, such as the F1000 single-seater cars, a championship we will discuss in the next section.

If you do decide to invest in a pop-up awning, always have the sides available, too, they are particularly useful when the rain comes – when racing in the UK you can bet on having at least a few wet races per season. Whilst mentioning the weather, it's useful to have your ratchet straps to hand, as you can use them to secure your pop-up awning to your trailer and your car. This is just an extra precaution in case of strong winds, but it's a useful tip. An alternative is to make use of any large tubs you may have lying around. Take these with you to a race meeting, fill them with water and use them as weights for your awning, again attached by ratchet straps.

Another consideration is electricity. If you are based in a pit garage you will more than likely have access to power. The exception here being Thruxton, as the garages do not have a power supply. So it is always worth having a back-up option for times when you are not in a garage. There are also some circuits in the UK that do not have garages, so you will be based out in the open. These circuits include Mallory Park in Leicestershire, Castle Combe in Wiltshire and Knockhill in Scotland.

For those drivers based in the open air, do not worry, the majority of circuits have power at various points throughout the paddock. Circuits such as Brands Hatch, Donington Park, Thruxton and Oulton Park, to name just a few, have electricity points around the surrounding edge of the paddock. Just be aware that there may be a charge for this power, and sometimes circuits will not turn the power on until that unit has been paid for, so be prepared for this. Your organising club may well take up this expense, paying for any additional electricity point costs in advance.

You will need the appropriate cable to connect to these electric points, of course. A long cable is advisable, as you're unlikely to be based right next to the main point. Your cable will need a 16 amp plug on one end to be able to connect to the electric hook-up point. You can get these cables with the same sort of connector on the other end, alternatively, you can get a set of three pin plug sockets on the other end, ready to plug your kettle straight into. Depending on where you shop, for a cable such as this you would be looking at spending between £30 and £40. It is worth having a source of power, not just for the all-important kettle, but for any electric tools you may need to use during the weekend, or even a heater on those cold days.

If you are unable to reach the electricity points at a circuit, or you are racing at a circuit without any electric hook-up access, the other option is a generator. Whether you buy this or borrow one from a friend, this is something you will need to supply yourself. You can hire generators that will be delivered to the circuit for you, but consider the associated cost. Once you have made friends in the paddock, it may be something that you can split the cost of between you and a few other drivers.

With track days, you will likely have garage access, if the circuit allows for it, but this will often come at an additional cost. Some companies will offer free garages on a first-come first-served basis, whereas other track day organisers will charge for a garage. Either way, if you can afford the extra expense, when booking your track day place it is often worth booking a garage as well, particularly if the weather forecast is rather dismal. That way you have a warm, dry environment in which to spend the day, and access to electricity should you need it.

With club level motorsport, always plan to set up in the open paddock: that way you will always have all the equipment you could ever need, and won't be caught out.

As daft as it may sound, another essential item I have already mentioned is a kettle. If you are a tea or coffee drinker this is definitely an important piece of equipment, and one that will make you many friends within the paddock. It may also be useful to have a coolbox on hand for cold drinks, milk, food: everything you could need during a weekend away from home. Whilst on the subject of food and drinks, it is also worth pointing out that you may want to bring your own food with you. Those who have come from karting and been a spectator at race meetings will be aware of the food situation at the various circuits, in terms of what is and isn't available. However, those who are new to motorsport need to be prepared. The price and quality of food at race circuits varies greatly. Some circuits may only supply a burger van, which may be fine for some, but for those who suffer with nerves before a race, a burger is probably not the best meal before jumping into a race car. Other circuits, such as the MotorSport

Vision venues, have a restaurant on site, with a variety of hot and cold meals, snacks and drinks available, catering for breakfast, lunch and evening meals. Although many circuits have restaurant facilities on site, consider the cost, as it can make the weekend even more expensive. Another benefit of having access to electricity is that you can easily supply your own food and drinks, to help manage outgoing costs. Although the majority of circuits do not stop this, it may be prohibited at some venues – this information should be included in the final instructions sent prior to each race meeting.

Now you are armed with the essential items to get you through a race weekend, let's move on to the different championships and series.

Championships and series

When you start looking at the championships or series to join, it can seem somewhat overwhelming. There is definitely a lot to choose from, but the race car you choose will help determine your preferred championship or series, or at least narrow it down. Begin by looking at the different organising clubs, to see which events they run and what sort of competition might suit your preferred race car. Once you start to break it down, you will begin to develop a clearer picture, especially if you already have a car in mind. You will also discover that your car will likely be eligible for multiple events run by the different clubs; for instance, those who race in the 750 Motor Club Roadsports Series will often race in the Club's Club Enduro Championship or Hot Hatch Championship as well, often during the same weekend. Racing in different championships under the same club can have its advantages. Although you will have significant outgoings to consider, you will also enjoy maximum track time by squeezing as much as possible into two days.

There are championships and series that offer multi-class racing, such as the Roadsports Series, Hot Hatch Championship or Sport Specials, and there are one-make championships, such as the various Caterham Motorsport championships, the Caterham Graduates Racing Club, the Fiesta Championship or the Locost Championship, each run by different clubs. People often prefer the one-make option, as each driver on-circuit is in the same sort of car, levelling the field somewhat. Whichever you choose, you will have fun and enjoy a competitive battle, regardless of where you are on the grid.

Junior racing championships and series

If you are a junior racing driver, you are more limited on what you can compete in. Junior championships are eligible for drivers between 14-17 years. Despite the limited availability, there is a strong calibre of championships in existence, with many drivers progressing to much bigger things within the motorsport industry.

Starting at the more budget-friendly end of the scale, there is the Junior Saloon Car Championship (JSCC), open to drivers aged between 14 and 17. Housing cars such as a 1600 Citroën Saxo VTR, the championship offers fun, close racing for young drivers looking to enjoy their first foray into motorsport. The JSCC operates under the British Automobile Racing Club (BARC), one of the longest standing motor racing clubs in the UK. We will discuss the different clubs in the next section.

Another good quality, affordable junior championship is the Fiesta Junior Championship. Again, a popular feeder series for those drivers looking to progress through the ranks, the Fiesta Junior Championship has flourished a great deal in recent years. It now boasts very competitive grids and is another cost-friendly championship. This championship operates under the British Racing and Sports Car Club (BRSCC), another established club within British motorsport.

Finally, set at the higher end of the budget scale, is the higher profile Ginetta Junior Championship. Ginetta Cars has established itself as one of the biggest names in motorsport. From its Yorkshire base, the company now has an army of cars and championships, from the Ginetta Junior Championship through to British GT Championship feeder championships and LMP1 machines. Aimed at drivers who are in the same age bracket, 14-16 years of age, the Ginetta junior Championship welcomes those who are embarking on their first taste of motorsport. Drivers may finish the championship at 17 years of age, however, as long as they are 16 years old when they begin the season, they are still permitted to enter. Given the high-profile nature of the championship, for instance its position on the British Touring Car Championship (BTCC) package and live televised races on ITV4, it is a popular competition, however it comes with a much higher budget.

Upon graduating from a junior championship, drivers are permitted to apply for a senior, or normal, race licence. As a young racing driver, learning your race craft in the junior ranks has its benefits, but it is not essential. Once you reach 16 years of age you are permitted to apply for a regular race licence; this will entitle you to compete in an array of championships and series across the UK. There are many routes into becoming a racing driver, some young drivers will begin in karting before progressing to car racing in their later teenage years, some will begin in one of the various junior championships from the age of 14, whereas others may head straight into one of the many club level championships on offer, once they are old enough. Choose the route that suits you, your time and budget.

Senior racing championships and series

From the age of 16 you are classed as a 'senior' racing driver, and therefore once you are armed with your ARDS licence, the motor racing world is your oyster.

SO, YOU WANT TO BE A RACING DRIVER?

There is an abundance of championships and series within the UK, each fitting a varying level of budget, ability, and experience, and many of which are ideal for absolute beginners, regardless of starting age.

Some championships and series are easy for a novice driver to jump into from the off, others can be a baptism of fire. It all depends on the competitive level of the grid you are joining, but all clubs would like to be considered as novice friendly. In the Clubs section, following this, you will notice each club generally has novice-friendly championships, as well as those that are more high-profile and suited to the more experienced racer, presenting you with a good progression route.

There are some opportunities to join a novice-specific level of competition. For instance, in 2011 Want2Race (covered in more detail in Chapter 3 under 'Track days') launched what is now the biggest novice racing driver competition in the UK. In a bid to encourage new drivers, the competition offers its lucky winner a fully funded season in the Ginetta G40 Cup. Open to aspiring racing drivers over the age of 18, the competition sees drivers compete throughout three stages to find the winner.

Rather than relying on winning a competition, there are, of course, other opportunities for rookie racers to get on track in a novice-friendly environment, one option being the Type R Trophy Foundation. Organised under the 750 Motor Club banner, the Foundation was launched towards the end of 2020 in a bid to welcome new drivers to UK motorsport. There are two options available within the Type R Trophy Foundation, one for a complete novice, and one aimed at current motorsport licence holders. The novice package includes:

➤ Go Racing starter pack (which includes the cost of your first race licence)
➤ ARDS test
➤ Medical
➤ Full race kit – helmet, HANS device, race suit, gloves, boots, and a balaclava
➤ Instructor session at the Club's pre-season track day
➤ A fully built ready-to-race Honda Civic Type R race car, which is yours to keep
➤ A second pair of tyres and a second set of brake pads
➤ A pre-season track day
➤ 12 months' membership with the 750 Motor Club
➤ Registration fee for the TEGIWA Type R Trophy
➤ Six double-header race meeting (12 races in total)
➤ Transponder hire for all six race meetings
➤ Discounted mechanical support and spares from Motion Motorsport

The price for the Novice package (based on the 2021 season) is £11,995, which is superb value. The licence holder package includes everything except the Go Racing pack, a race licence and ARDS test, a medical, full race kit and free instruction during the pre-season track day. This package costs £10,495.

For those focused on the single-seater route, there are a number of entry-level single-seater championships, ideal for those racing at club level. I will go through some of them here, to give you an idea of what's available.

First up there is the Monoposto Championship. Organised under the MotorSport Vision Racing (MSVR) brand, the Monoposto Championship offers friendly, affordable yet competitive racing. One of the longer standing single-seater clubs, the Monoposto Championship has been part of the motorsport community since 1958. Attracting capacity grids on a regular basis, the championship is popular with those amongst the club motor racing scene in the UK.

With a large emphasis on amateur racing drivers, the Monoposto championship is an ideal proving ground to learn your way around a single-seater race car. There are various classes available, with the engine size of your car determining which class you are eligible for. In order to maintain its cost-effective ethos, cars must be at least four years old to be able to compete. Although all cars competing in the Monoposto Championship are manufactured to a high standard, some of the classes, such as Mono Moto 1400 and 1000 lend themselves to those who prefer to build their own cars. The inclusive nature of the championship means that those who do opt for the self-build route in these respective classes can still be just as competitive as those who purchase a ready-to-race machine.

The different Monoposto Championship classes include:

➤ Mono F3
➤ Mono 2000
➤ Mono 2000 Classic
➤ Mono 1800
➤ Mono 1600
➤ Mono Moto 1000
➤ Mono Moto 1400

The two Mono Moto classes are for motorcycle-engined cars. Cars that race in all classes (apart from the Mono Moto classes that are built commercially) must be built for the 2006 season or earlier.

To register with the Monoposto Championship, the cost is £145, which includes a £45 membership fee, plus £100 to register as a driver for the championship, making it very cost effective indeed. Don't forget you will need to pay your individual race entry fees on top of that; these can range from £320 to £470 per round, depending on the circuit and the amount of races included.

SO, YOU WANT TO BE A RACING DRIVER?

As with all car racing, different championships can differ greatly on their registration and race entry fees.

Another single-seater championship to consider is Formula Vee. This is a long-standing championship with a history that goes back more than 50 years, and is a good breeding ground boasting strong entry lists round after round. Run by the 750 Motor Club, the Formula Vee Championship is another club level budget-friendly competition.

With a 1300cc air-cooled VW type 1/2/3 engine housed in the single-seater chassis, the Formula Vee is a competitive car. Engine power tends to be around the 85bhp mark, with average lap speeds within the 90-95mph bracket. Costs incurred with registration total £160, which breaks down into a £25 club membership fee plus £135 registration fee. Additional costs to expect on top of this will include race entries; these are usually between £250 and £350 per round. Cars that are eligible for the Formula Vee Championship can be sourced secondhand for around £5000.

F1000 is an accessible single-seater championship that also runs under the 750 Motor Club banner. Dubbed the UK's premier motorcycle-engined single-seater series, F1000 has flourished since its inception back in 1997. Suitable for novice racing drivers or those with a little more experience, the championship offers an affordable step onto the single-seater ladder, particularly to those coming into the sport from karting. This 'slicks and wings' pure race car is powered by a 1000cc bike engine. With grid numbers usually upwards of 20 cars, there is plenty of competition throughout the field. The championship also features a full supply of spare parts, as well as technical support, at each round.

Fees associated with joining the F1000 Championship differ, depending on which registration you choose. The different options include:

➤ Annual Championship Class registration – £225
➤ Annual Formula Jedi – £140
➤ Guest registration (for a single event) – £50

There is an additional charge of £25, which covers 12 months of membership for the 750 Motor Club. For those competitors racing in the F1000 Championship in 2021, organisers offered drivers a £30 discount on their registration fee. In order to claim this, competitors had to have been part of the championship during the previous season, and register and pay by a certain date. It is worth keeping an eye on information from your respective championship or series, as they will often offer incentives, such as an early-bird registration discount.

There are a number of Formula Ford championships that also offer competitive single-seater experience. Some of these will be more budget friendly than others. Starting at the more cost-effective end of the scale there is the

Formula Ford 1600 category. Organised under the watchful eye of the BRSCC (all organising clubs will be discussed in the next section), Formula Ford 1600 was created over 50 years ago, and is still going strong. Incorporated under the Formula Ford 1600 banner are various individual championships, including:

> **National FF1600**
> This competition is described as the best entry level single-seater championship
> **Northern and Super Classic**
> Aimed at the clubman racing driver, this series focuses on the North and Midlands in the UK, with events taking place at Mallory Park, Oulton Park and Anglesey
> **Single venue series**
> This series encompasses competitions at either Oulton Park or Mallory Park, with its Champion of Oulton and Star of Mallory events

National FF1600 has produced some very successful single-seater racers, with drivers progressing to the likes of British F4, British Formula 3 and beyond, proving its worth as a competitive single-seater feeder programme. Many former Formula One World Champions also began their car racing careers in Formula Ford, with names such as Ayrton Senna and Nigel Mansell amongst that impressive list.

For those based in Scotland there is the Scottish Formula Ford 1600 Championship. Organised and run by the Scottish Motor Racing Club (SMRC), this championship is centred around the Knockhill circuit, with one away round taking place at Cadwell Park. Although it may seem unusual to mainly use one circuit for a sole championship, the unique thing about Knockhill is its ability to run race meetings both clockwise and anti-clockwise: a very rare occurrence, with only a very small number of circuits able to run like this. Given the undulating nature of the Scottish circuit, it is an incredible and unique experience.

Upon mentioning the SMRC, this is a good opportunity to note that joining the Club, as well as being affordable, has a number of other advantages. These include 15% discount from the full Torq race wear range, and 10% discount on HEL Performance braided clutch and brake hoses with PerformanceTek, amongst other useful benefits.

There are also some classic and historic Formula Ford Championships that will appeal to a certain type of racing driver. Although these championships will give you the necessary experience of racing a single-seater race car, it may be a slightly different option for those looking at a more professional single-seater route.

SO, YOU WANT TO BE A RACING DRIVER?

As you begin to advance through the single-seater ranks, as with tin top racing, the budget will increase as the championship reaches a higher profile status. An example of such a championship is British F4. Certified by the FIA (Fédération Internationale de l'Automobile), the governing body behind motorsport such as Formula One, the British F4 Championship is the first step on the FIA single-seater programme for drivers hoping to reach the realms of Formula One. The championship is thought of as an affordable step before reaching the dizzying heights of British Formula 3, with a budget to reflect this. In order to effectively manage the budget needed for the F4 Championship, the cost of a new chassis has been kept to a minimum, with an additional thought given to the price of consumables to help reduce costs.

The British F4 Championship is open to drivers from the age of 15 who hold the correct ARDS race licence. To give you an idea of how the cost differs at this level, registration for the British F4 Championship costs £2500, plus a further £11,000 to enter all rounds for a full season campaign. For those wanting to enter round by round, the entry fee is £1500 (plus VAT on all prices). In terms of the car, these are often available secondhand for around the £16,500 mark, however this can differ greatly from seller to seller, and it will also depend on whether the car comes with any spare parts or tyres, for instance. Alternatively, some teams involved in the championship may offer an arrive-and-drive package.

During the next section, not only will I discuss the various motorsport clubs we have here in the UK, but also the championships that each club hosts. Let's delve in.

The clubs

Once you select the championship or series you wish to contest, you will need to join a club. Each championship is attached to an organising club, and I recommend researching the clubs as much as the individual championships, as each one will operate slightly differently. There are a number of motor and motorsport clubs to consider joining, all of whom organise race meetings and events throughout the UK. As a nice bonus, some also run a token European race meeting at circuits such as Spa Francorchamps, Zandvoort or Zolder. The opportunity to visit some of the European circuits should not be missed if possible. Racing at Spa Francorchamps is definitely a box that needs ticking.

Some of the clubs listed below are more specialist than others, which will be fairly evident from the club's name, such as the vintage and historic groups. There are also some clubs that fall under the umbrella of those listed below, for example the Caterham Graduates Racing Club is a championship that operates under the BARC banner, so it is worth investigating each further to see just what it is they have to offer. Some of the main organising clubs include:

> 750 Motor Club
> British Automobile Racing Club (BARC)
> British Racing and Sports Car Club (BRSCC)
> Classic Sports Car Club (CSCC)
> Historic Sports Car Club (HSCC)
> MG Car Club (MGCC)
> MotorSport Vision Racing (MSVR)
> Vintage Sports Car Club (VSCC)

Each of these organisations coordinate and run their own events. Although bound by regulations set by Motorsport UK, each organising club will set out their own rules surrounding event booking and payments, as well as the supplementary regulations connected to each championship or series.

You may have the opportunity to sample the different clubs, depending on the championship or series you sign up to. There are some smaller clubs and series who will join the main clubs listed above for selected race meetings. Some may even split their calendar between a few of them, entering a race meeting as a guest championship. If you have signed up to one particular club, having the chance to race with another club is a great opportunity to experience different racing and organisation, so you really get to see what else is available.

So, you have carried out endless research and finally narrowed down your choice of championship. Once you have finalised your choice, you will need to become a member of your chosen club, as well as register for the championship or series. Apart from being essential from an insurance* point of view (*insurance for the club, you will need to organise your own racing insurance if you decide you want it), joining a club has added benefits. For instance, with regard to the 750 Motor Club, membership entitles you to the Club's member discounts, which include discounts from various trade suppliers, as well as 10% off at Demon Tweeks. If you still have some items of your race kit to buy, this 10% discount could be very useful. BARC offers a host of member benefits, including the opportunity to compete in over 30 Motorsport UK registered championships, the club's informative quarterly club magazine, a discounted subscription to *Autosport* magazine, discounted admission to events at Thruxton circuit and an end of year season review, amongst much more. The BRSCC membership benefits include a free ticket to the *Autosport* International Racing Car Show, which runs across four days in January each year, a complimentary ticket to a select number of BRSCC race events, plus a host of discounted rates on items purchased through the BRSCC store.

Now I have discussed the basics, let's delve further into each of these clubs. You will notice similarities between some of the championships and series organised by each club. As you can imagine there is always an element of competition between the clubs, to appear the most attractive to prospective racing drivers. Don't forget, once you have joined a club you will also need to register for your chosen championship.

- 750 Motor Club

Some clubs may offer a flat membership rate for the year, whereas others may give you the option of varying levels of membership, based on what you intend to race or your experience level. Nice and simply, the 750 Motor Club (750MC) has one membership price: £25 for 12 months. For this, you can either become a racing member, a sporting trials member, or an Austin 7 member. Now in its 82nd year (2021), the 750 Motor Club knows how to organise and look after championships and series. Dubbed 'the home of affordable motorsport,' the 750MC is an ideal place for drivers to begin their racing career. Although the 750MC doesn't host a junior championship, it will accept drivers with a full ARDS licence from the age of 16. With a total of 23 championships and series from single-seaters to hot hatches currently organised and run by the Club, there is certainly plenty of choice for new and more experienced drivers.

Although each will run under the 750MC banner, many of the associated championships and series operate on a day-to-day basis under a respective coordinator. This is the case for the majority of championships and series, regardless of the organising club. The coordinator will usually act as a representative for the drivers, taking the position of go-between between you and the club.

The current list of formulae includes:

➤ 116 Trophy
➤ 750 Formula Championship (the world's oldest continually running race series)
➤ Alfa Romeo Championship
➤ Armed Forces Challenge
➤ Bernie's Sports Racing & V8s
➤ Bikesports Championship
➤ BMW Car Club Racing Championship
➤ CALM All Porsche Trophy
➤ Classic Stock Hatch Championship
➤ Clio 182 Championship
➤ Club Enduro Championship
➤ F1000 Championship
➤ Formula Vee
➤ Historic 750 Formula
➤ Hot Hatch Championship
➤ Locost Championship

➤ Ma7da Championship
➤ MX-5 Cup Championship
➤ Roadsports Series
➤ Sports 1000 Championship
➤ Sport Specials Championship
➤ Toyota MR2 Championship
➤ Type R Trophy

Registration fee for the championships and series within the 750MC ranges from £50 for the Bernie's Sports Racing and V8s series, to £150 for the likes of the Club Enduro Championship, the Toyota MR2 Championship and the BMW Car Club Racing Championship, with plenty of options in between. This registration fee entitles you to a full season, with individual race entry fees on top that you will pay as you go along. The 750MC also offers a single event registration, which costs just £25. You can register for any of the Club's championships or series for just £25, entitling you to enter just one race. If you decide you would like to enter more races within that championship or series after this, you can upgrade to the full registration by paying the remaining balance. This is quite a nice way to introduce yourself to a championship or series, with a one event 'taster'. (There is still the normal entry fee on top of the £25 registration fee.)

As well as its regular catalogue of championships and series, the 750MC is also responsible for the Birkett Six Hour Relay. As the name suggests, it is a six-hour endurance race that takes place in October every year. The perfect end of season treat, the Birkett welcomes all manner of cars and drivers from championships across the UK, and with 70 grid places available, it never fails to reach capacity. Teams are usually made up of three to six cars, with the race operating in a relay fashion. In 2021, the Birkett Relay celebrated its 71st year.

• BARC
The BARC is another of the UK's resident motorsport clubs incorporating different centres across the UK. Unlike the 750 Motor Club, the BARC offers different membership options,including:

➤ **Club Membership – £40**
Club members are entitled to carry the BARC badge, reap many of the club benefits and become further involved in the club, by training to become an official or marshal.
➤ **Racing Membership – £145**
This membership is specifically open to members who are racing in one of the BARC organised championships.

SO, YOU WANT TO BE A RACING DRIVER?

I hereby apply for membership of the 750 Motor Club Limited and agree to be bound by the Memorandum & Articles of Association of the Company.

Title (Mr/Mrs/Miss/Ms/Dr):

Forename/s:

Surname:

Address:

Home 'phone: Work 'phone:

Mobile 'phone:

Email :

Date of Birth:

Application form for the 750 Motor Club.

Membership Application Form

Annual Membership **£25**

What is your main interest? (please tick only one box)

Austin 7 ☐   Trials ☐   Racing ☐

750 Motor Club Austin 7 Register

If you are the Registered Keeper of an Austin Seven and would like the details included on the A7CA register of cars owned by A7 Club Members worldwide, please complete the details overleaf, if necessary continuing on a separate sheet.
This will entitle you to receive a free copy of the A7CA magazine.

Please send the completed form to:

750 Motor Club, Western Paddock, Donington Park, Castle Donington, Derbyshire DE74 2RP.
Membership@750MC.co.uk
☎: 01332 814548 📠: 01332 811422

The Seven-Fifty Motor Club Ltd. Registered in England & Wales - number 552948
Registered Office: Western Paddock, Donington Park, Castle Donington, Derby DE74 2RP

WWW.750MC.CO.UK

PAYMENT INFORMATION

I have enclosed a cheque for the required amount. ☐

I will contact the club office directly to pay by credit card. ☐

I will pay by BACS transfer (see details below). ☐
Sort Code: 20-14-33 Account Number: 40860786

> **Centre Memberships** – £15 each
> This is for those members who wish to join one of the various BARC centres around the UK. This is an additional fee on top of Club Membership and entitles the holder to contest that centre's competitive events. Those members wishing to contest Hillclimb and Sprint events under a specific centre only need to apply for this membership for their respective centre.

> **Joint Membership** – £10
> If you are already a BARC member, your spouse or partner can join for just £10.

> **Junior Membership** (10-17 years) – £7
> Entitles the member to carry the BARC badge. A junior member will

also receive copies of the Club's quarterly magazine, and be entitled to discounted entry to events at Thruxton Circuit.

Each of the above will include different features and benefits, depending on the level of membership you choose.

There is an eclectic mix of championships that run under the BARC banner. In contrast to the 750MC, BARC hosts everything from high-profile events to the more entry-level club championships, as you will see from the following list. In keeping with the theme of this book, I will start at the lower end of the spectrum:

➤ Car racing championships
  ➢ Caterham Graduates Racing Club
  ➢ BARC Red
  ➢ One Litre Racing Club
  ➢ Hyundai Coupé Cup
  ➢ Max5 Racing Championship
  ➢ Junior Saloon Car Championship
  ➢ 2CV Championship
  ➢ Sports/Saloon Car Championship
  ➢ Mighty Minis Championship
  ➢ Kumho BMW Championship
  ➢ MG Owners' Club Championship
  ➢ Sports Prototype Cup
  ➢ Citroën C1 Racing Series
  ➢ Classic Touring Car Racing Club (CTCRC) – various championships
  ➢ Legends Cars National Championship
  ➢ British Touring Car Championship (BTCC) and its support package
  ➢ Ginetta G40 Cup
  ➢ Ginetta GT5 Challenge
  ➢ Ginetta Junior Championship
  ➢ Ginetta GT4 Supercup
  ➢ Porsche Carrera Cup GB
  ➢ Ginetta GT Academy
  ➢ Porsche Sprint Challenge GB
  ➢ Mini Challenge
➤ Hillclimb and speed events
  ➢ Harewood Speed Hillclimb Championship
  ➢ Gurston Down Speed Hillclimb Championship
  ➢ British Hillclimb Championship
  ➢ BARC Speed Championship

➤ Truck racing
- ➢ British Truck Racing Championship
- ➢ Pickup Truck Racing Championship

• **BRSCC**

As with the 750 Motor Club and the BARC, the BRSCC also hosts a multitude of championships and series, each welcoming various levels of ability and experience. Similarly to BARC, the BRSCC offers varying levels of club membership. Membership options include:

➤ Club membership – £45
➤ Racing membership – £150
➤ Junior membership – £12.50
➤ Guest racing membership – £50

In terms of championships on offer, the BRSCC hosts everything from saloon and production cars, to single-seaters, sports cars and GT and touring machines. Championships that run under the BRSCC label include the following. As with BARC, the BRSCC hosts a number of high-profile competitions, so again I have started with the most cost-effective options:

➤ Clubsport Trophy
➤ Fiesta Junior Championship
➤ Fiesta Championship
➤ Mazda MX-5:
- ➢ Mazda MX-5 Championship
- ➢ Mazda MX-5 Clubman Championship
- ➢ Mazda MX-5 MK4 Trophy
- ➢ Mazda MX-5 Supercup
➤ Caterham Championships:
- ➢ Caterham Academy Championship
- ➢ Caterham Roadsports Championship
- ➢ Caterham 270R Championship
- ➢ Caterham 310R Championship
- ➢ Seven UK Championship
➤ ST-XR Challenge
➤ Supersport Endurance Cup
➤ BMW Compact Cup
➤ Citycar Cup Championship
➤ Track Attack Race Club
➤ Modified Ford Series

➤ Northern and Super Classic Formula Ford Championship
➤ National Formula Ford Championship
➤ Formula Ford Festival
➤ Fun Cup Endurance Championship
➤ Aston Martin Owners' Club (AMOC):
    ➢ AMOC GT Challenge
    ➢ AMOC Ireland Cup
    ➢ Intermarque Championship
    ➢ AMOC Jack Fairman Cup
    ➢ AMOC Prewar Team Challenge
    ➢ AMOC Aston Martin GT4 Challenge
➤ British GT Championship

As you can see there is a great deal of variety within the BRSCC, to suit all manner of budgets.

• **Classic Sports Car Club**
As the name suggests, the Classic Sports Car Club (CSCC), is open to cars that fall into the realm of being considered a classic. Membership with the CSCC is pretty simple, it costs £39 for 12 months from the date of joining. Nice and straightforward. You will need to pay a further £99 to register your car for a series within the CSCC, with a 50% reduction applied to your registration fee if you opt to join more than one series.

With a total of 12 series to choose from, the CSCC is on a slightly smaller scale to that of those clubs previously mentioned, yet it offers fun, affordable racing at every turn. The series you can expect to enjoy with the CSCC include:

➤ Classic K Series (pre-1966 cars running to appendix K)
➤ Swinging '60s Series (cars from the 1950s and 1960s)
➤ Future Classics Series (cars from the 1970s and 1980s)
➤ Special Saloons and Modsports Series (cars up to 1993)
➤ Modern Classics Series (cars produced up to the end of 1999)
➤ New Millennium Series (post year 2000 production-based cars and their racing variants)
➤ Tin Tops Series (hot hatchbacks and saloons, four-cylinder, naturally-aspirated)
➤ Turbo Tin Tops Series (turbo and supercharged front-wheel-drive cars)
➤ Magnificent Sevens Series (cars based on the Lotus Seven design, including Caterham)
➤ Mazda RX08 Trophy (road legal, first generation 2002-2008)
➤ Open Series (saloons, hatchbacks, sports and GT cars with doors)

SO, YOU WANT TO BE A RACING DRIVER?

➤ Slicks Series (saloons, hatchbacks, sports and GT cars with doors, on slick or racing wet tyres)

• **Historic Sports Car Club**

Again, very self-explanatory the Historic Sports Car Club (HSCC) is aimed at those wishing to compete in the historic side of the sport. There are three levels of membership available for drivers wanting to join the HSCC:

➤ **Novice membership** – £195
  Novice members will also receive a voucher to the value of £200 towards the cost of their first entry fee with HSCC
➤ **Full Racing membership** – £195
  Entitles the member to compete in one or more championships per season
➤ **Basic Racing membership** – £70
  This membership allows for entry into a single event. The fee is refundable against an upgrade to full racing membership.

In terms of member benefits, the HSCC offers some desirable deals for its members, such as 10% discount with Demon Tweeks, 15% discount from Vital Equipment race apparel and safety equipment, 20% discount on regalia from Dread and discounted insurance policies with Hagerty Insurance.

Once signed up to the HSCC there is a great selection of championships and series available to enter with the HSCC, including:

➤ Aurora Trophy
➤ Guards Trophy
➤ Classic Formula 3
➤ Historic Touring Cars
➤ Historic Formula Junior
➤ '70s Road Sports
➤ Historic Formula Ford
➤ Historic Road Sports
➤ Historic Formula Ford 2000
➤ 1980s Production Car Challenge
➤ Historic Formula 3
➤ Saloon Car Cup
➤ Thundersports
➤ Historic Formula 2
➤ Geoff Lees Trophy
➤ Classic Formula Ford

- **MG Car Club**

Centred around the different models of MG road and race cars, the MG Car Club (MGCC) is slightly different to the clubs discussed already. It is a motor club foremost with a motorsport division, so it is very heavily involved in road cars as well as racing machines. With that, there is a selection of annual memberships on offer, such as:

➤ Single membership – £50
➤ Joint membership – £54
➤ Overseas single membership – £50
➤ Overseas joint membership – £54
➤ Young member (16-20 years) -£15
➤ Young member (21-24 years) – £30

With regard to championships, the MGCC houses an assorted mix:

➤ MG Trophy Championship
➤ MG Cup
➤ MG Metro Cup
➤ MG Midget and Sprite Challenge
➤ BCV8 Championship
➤ Cockshoot Cup

The MGCC also hosts MG Live, the largest MG event in the world, attracting members from UK and international bases. Usually held at Silverstone circuit, the venue is transformed into a festival of MG cars, with an abundance of racing action across a full weekend, car displays, musical entertainment, car demonstrations and auto tests.

- **MotorSport Vision Racing**

As a fan of motorsport you will no doubt be familiar with the MotorSport Vision brand. Owners of some of the most popular circuits in the UK, including Brands Hatch, Donington Park, Oulton Park, Snetterton, Cadwell Park and Bedford Autodrome, MotorSport Vision (MSV) also organise track days (MSV Track Days) and race meetings, MotorSport Vision Racing (MSVR).

Another club that boasts a vast collection of championships and series, from entry level sprint and endurance races through to the more prominent events, MSVR features some superb racing, and plenty of budget friendly options, such as:

➤ Circuit racing
  ➢ EnduroKA

- Focus Cup
- MotorSport Vision SuperCup
- MSVR All-Comers
- MSVT Trackday Trophy
- Production Golf and BMW Championship
- Toyo Tires 7 Race Series
- MSVR Elise Trophy Championship
- Sports 2000
- Monoposto Championship
- Porsche Club Championship
- Ferrari Challenge UK
- Heritage Formula Ford
- Champion of Brands
- Clubmans Sports Prototype Championship
- Radical SR1 Cup Championship
- Radical Challenge Championship
- 911 Challenge
- Mini Challenge Trophy
- F3 Cup Championship
- BRDC British F3 Championship
- GT Cup Championship
- Z Cars and New Generation Production BMW Championship

- Speed competition
  - Lotus Cup UK Speed Championship
  - Rally
  - Motorsport News Circuit Rally Championship

- **Vintage Sports Car Club**

Finally, we come to the Vintage Sports Car Club (VSCC). Another club that falls into the more specialist motorsport category, the VSCC offers some spectacular action, in some very special vintage machinery.

With a heritage that stretches back to 1934, the VSCC is still very much an active part of the motorsport fraternity. As with other clubs, the VSCC has a range of membership bundles available, each running from January to December, depending on what you wish to achieve with the club. Membership packages purchased on the VSCC website are also cheaper than contacting the office directly:

- **Vintage membership** – from £93
  For UK owners of pre-1931 cars
- **Driving membership** – from £93

For UK owners of certain post-vintage thoroughbred cars up to 1940 and certain historic racing cars

> **Associate membership** – from £93

For UK residents who do not currently own a prewar car

> **European membership** – from £110
> **Rest of world membership** – from £117
> **Junior memberships** – £10

For any members aged 16 and under

> **Young membership** – £50

For any members aged 17 and under

VSCC competition incorporates all manner of motor racing events, from hillclimbing to circuit racing, rallying and road tours.

Whichever club you decide to join, make sure you check the renewal date of your membership. You will most likely receive a reminder but be aware some memberships will run January to December, whereas others will run for 12 months from the date you first register.

Have a look at each club individually, to see which is best suited to you, in terms of cost, the membership options available and most importantly the championships they offer. Website addresses for each organisation can be found in Appendix 3.

CHAPTER 3

TRACK TIME

TRACK DAYS

So, you've got your race car. Now it's time to start using it.

You may be a novice racing driver when you take to the grid for your first outing, but that doesn't mean you are a complete novice when it comes to track action. Gaining experience on-circuit is important, especially if you are fairly apprehensive about the prospect, but it is easily achievable.

The best opportunity to get some practice on-circuit is with a track day or test day. First of all, track days and test days are very different events. Although you may use a track day as a test day, be aware that the event rules differ somewhat. For those set to become a car racing driver, track days are the most readily available opportunity to experience a circuit first-hand, and less daunting than jumping straight into a test day for your first time on-circuit. Although some more experienced racing drivers will use a track day as an opportunity to practise and prepare for an upcoming race, track days tend to attract less experienced or novice circuit drivers, making it a more friendly environment for someone new to racing or driving on-circuit. It is a very relaxed environment, making it the ideal training ground for novices looking to gain some experience.

Whether you plan to use your road car, or the car you intend to race, to prepare yourself for the real experience there are opportunities at circuits all over the UK and Europe to learn the circuit directly, before you turn up to race. Some track day companies also offer car hire, and although you don't have to worry about the level of wear and tear as you would on your own car, you will need to consider the cost implications of hiring a car. Yes, it will be somewhat expensive, but is it any more expensive than what you would have paid on fuel and tyres for your own car, plus the difficult job of getting the car to the circuit? Car hire can be a convenient option, but there may be more to consider in terms of cost or insurance cover.

Track days work a little differently in karting. Although kart track days are not as readily available, there are plenty of opportunities to get on-circuit at your local kart track or with your local club. As discussed in Chapter 2, venues such as Daytona Kart Circuit will offer ample opportunities to get some karting experience, either in your own kart or with an 'arrive and drive' package.

Taking your road car on a track day can be useful, especially if this is one of your first experiences of driving on-circuit. To start with, getting out on-circuit is about gaining experience and confidence, and learning the track. It's handy to know what's ahead, whether it's a tight right-hand turn or a long, fast left-hand turn, so a road car can be extremely helpful for this. Once you have navigated your way around the circuit and discovered which way it goes, it is more beneficial to take your race car on a track day, as your race car will handle very differently compared to your road car. Bear in mind that track days are geared up for closed wheel cars. Those wishing to take their single-seater race car on a track day will need to book a single-seater specific day, or a test day. A track day is also a steadier way of introducing yourself and your car to the track without the pressure of more experienced racing drivers hounding you. A pre-race weekend test day will likely be a bit more frantic, and will often be split into sessions, limiting the amount of time you have on-circuit.

Some championships can become quite cut-throat when it comes to track time, with drivers stealing away to bank some laps at every opportunity. For those with a smaller budget or tougher work commitments, this isn't always possible. You will find that the more competitive or high-profile the championship or series, the more drivers will be seeking every possible opportunity to test, in order to maintain a competitive edge. As a novice, it is all about the experience, finding your feet, and securing seat time as and when you can. It doesn't have to become an arms race, it can be a more budget-friendly activity, so don't worry if you can't quite keep up with how much track time some drivers are experiencing. There will always be plenty of others you are racing against who are in the same position as you.

Booking a track day

In terms of requirements for booking a track day, it couldn't be simpler; you just need a road driving licence to be able to take part. You must show your road driving licence to be able to sign on for a track day, as a race licence will not be accepted. Junior drivers aged 14-16 obviously won't have a driving licence, but don't worry, they can still take part. We will discuss this in more detail below.

There are a number of respected and well-known track day companies in the industry, all of which host regular events throughout the year, from January to December, at circuits all over the UK. Although there tends to be a standard format when it comes to track day organisation, each company will offer variations in terms of prices, dates, the choice of circuits available, and the sort of day it is, for instance silenced or unsilenced, open pit lane or sessions. Before booking your track day, be aware that there may be restrictions in place that could affect the car you plan to take (such as noise restrictions), but this is explained in more detail throughout this section.

All track day organisers will be able to offer dates at the more prominent circuits within the UK, such as Donington Park, Silverstone, Brands Hatch and Oulton Park, to name just a few, but if you delve slightly deeper you will see that some organisations will run events at smaller circuits, such as Blyton Park and Mallory Park. Available track days at some circuits will be extremely limited, largely due to noise restrictions. Circuit organisers have to be mindful of the local communities surrounding their venue, in order to remain operational. Although circuits such as Blyton Park don't hold race meetings, it is a popular driver development and test circuit. Sometimes it is just as important to drive your car on-circuit and secure some seat time, especially if your experience of this is limited or non-existent. You will often find Blyton Park hosts quieter days, in terms of numbers, which is a great confidence booster. You are likely to find some very interesting cars in the paddock, with everything from club level racers to historic Formula One cars.

In terms of costs, you will find track days to be very seasonal, for instance, events that take place towards the beginning of the year and towards the end of the year will be cheaper, as the weather and lack of light are likely to reduce the amount of track time available, whereas a day at Brands Hatch or Silverstone in the middle of summer has a big draw and will likely be priced at the higher end of the scale. Prices per track day will differ between companies as well. Some days may seem rather expensive, but it may guarantee a better quality of track time. Basically, each organisation will be charged the same price to hire a circuit, but some companies will take more bookings than others. The more bookings a track day company takes, the cheaper the day will be, but that also means the day will be much busier due to a greater number of cars on the day. Each circuit has a limit for the number of cars they can allow on track at once, so for busy days that welcome a higher volume of bookings, be prepared to queue in the pit lane before going out on-circuit. You may not always have to queue, but it is worth being aware of it. If you prefer to book a day that will inevitably include less bookings, be prepared to pay a higher fee. The track day organisers that sit at the more premium end of the track day scale will be discussed in the information to come in this chapter, under 'Track day companies.'

A number of track day companies will also offer evening sessions that will take place during the spring and summer months when we're treated to extra daylight hours. More often than not, an evening session will allow for 2½ to 3½ hours of track time, usually between the hours of 5pm and 8:30pm, perfect for those drivers looking to bank some laps after work, especially if you just want to give your car a quick shakedown before its next outing. An evening session is also easier on the budget, in terms of the cost for the track time, fuel and tyres.

Many, if not all, track day companies within the UK will offer a number of additional extras; these are best added to your order during the booking process. Some track day organisers will offer car hire (as mentioned above), and although this can seem quite expensive, the cost of car hire will also include the track day fee, insurance and usually some instruction. When you work out the cost of each of these things separately it will put the amount into perspective. Other extras may include sessions of instruction in your own car, something that I cannot recommend enough. Spending a day with a qualified instructor on-circuit, either in your race car or your road car, is invaluable and definitely worth allocating some of your racing budget to. I have known many track day drivers who have been pounding round circuits all over the UK and Europe for years and years, without instruction. After suddenly deciding to pay for a session of professional advice, it was revolutionary for them. You may think those drivers who just stick to track days, and are not setting lap times or racing, don't need tuition, but they still want to learn how to drive a circuit in the best and quickest way possible, and instruction is one of the best ways to do this.

Different track day organisers will use different grades of instructor. Instructors do have racing experience, and upon becoming an instructor they are graded based on their level of experience. From the lowest grade of licence an instructor can hold to the most qualified, instructor grades are as follows:

> Grade C (probationary)
> Grade C
> Grade B (probationary)
> Grade B
> Grade A
> Grade S

Instructors of Grade A or S level are the most highly qualified and generally the most experienced, with chief instructors usually holding one of these grades. Some track day companies may only employ the highest grade of instructor, whereas others will open their doors to all qualified instructors, even those at probationary level. Prices for instruction will differ between different track day organisers, some may even offer free instruction sessions. As with road driving instructors, each race instructor works in a different way, it may suit your learning style, it may not. Once you have had your first tuition session, you may immediately find an instructor you work well with, and so book with them for future track days; they may even become your driver coach for test and race days. Building a relationship with your instructor can be vital, as you are putting an awful lot of trust in them when you're on-circuit, so you need to have confidence in one another.

Instead of booking sessions with an instructor through the organising company, you could book an independent instructor to accompany you for the day. There are very many qualified instructors in the motorsport industry, all of whom have racing experience, although some are more experienced than others. Over the years I have been fortunate enough to work with some of the best instructors in the country, all of whom I would happily recommend. Some driver coaches will work more with novice drivers, whilst others will work with all experience levels. During a race meeting, some will stay with you for the test day only, whereas others will stay throughout the weekend to help with data after qualifying for your races, it depends on your agreement with them. Most are included in the Instructor Directory in Appendix 4.

Booking an instructor for a track day can be very beneficial, obviously because it is a good opportunity to learn the circuit and the best racing lines, but it is also useful as your instructor can sit in-car with you. Having your instructor beside you is the best way to learn, as they can give instructions from the passenger seat. Although having a second person in the car will change the balance and speed around the circuit, it is the best way to learn, especially for novice drivers who just purely want to learn about braking zones and the best way to take a corner.

I will discuss data logging and lap timing equipment in Chapter 4, as I wouldn't want to associate it with track day information. With that in mind, this is the ideal time to mention one of the main rules to remember on track days: timing is not allowed. This is an extremely important point to remember. Track days are non-competitive events, so timing can invalidate the track day organiser's insurance. If you are caught timing, it could potentially end your day a lot sooner than you would like, so be careful not to have your timing equipment turned on. If you take anyone with you to a track day, also make sure they are not discreetly timing you from the pit wall. Believe me, track day organisers have seen all the tricks, and are wise to them all.

Additional services you may find available from your track day organiser include professional photography. Who doesn't want a photo of themselves driving their car on-circuit? Especially from their first track day, it is definitely exciting. Just remember that photographs are usually distributed following a track day event with little or no editing. If you are using your road car for a track day, one of the best pieces of advice I can give is to either tape up or remove your number plate prior to going out on-circuit. Again, drawing on my own experiences of working for a track day company, we encountered all manner of issues when the event photos had been released. For instance, if you are meant to be at work or you may have issues with your car insurance, make sure your number plate is not visible on photographs. The internet is an extremely small place.

Refreshments may be offered by your track day organiser. Some will offer complimentary tea and coffee, and maybe some biscuits if you are really lucky. Not all organisers will do this, but some will include it in your track day.

All track days can be found online, either on each respective track day company's website, or via a central hub, such as www.trackdays.co.uk. Booking directly with the organising company does have its advantages, such as ensuring you have the correct details for the day, and the option to contact the company should you need to. This is particularly useful if you are unable to attend and wish to request a refund.

Junior drivers

Track day requirements for junior drivers may differ between organisers. For example, some companies may insist the junior driver must have a qualified ARDS instructor, preferably of a higher grade, such as A or S, in the car with them at all times whilst on-circuit, and they must be using the car in which they intend to race. This is largely due to the insurance requirements held by the organising company. Companies such as MotorSport Vision (MSV) organise a Young Driver event, for 14- to 16-year-olds, for those yet to acquire a race licence. Most of you reading this will no doubt already know the MotorSport Vision brand and the experiences it offers. For those who don't know, MSV also owns some of the most prominent circuits in the UK, including Brands Hatch, Donington Park, Oulton Park, Snetterton and Cadwell Park, as well as Bedford Autodrome. If you're not yet aware of MSV, you soon will be. The best advice if you are booking a track day place for a junior driver is to double-check the requirements with the respective company prior to booking to avoid disappointment on the day.

If you are a junior driver attending a track or test day, you will need to have a parent or guardian with you, to countersign your indemnity form.

European days

When you first begin racing, your Clubman licence will only permit you to race on UK-based circuits. However, once rid of your novice status you may find yourself faced with the opportunity to race in Europe.

Many, but not all, racing clubs may have at least one European round listed on their calendar throughout the race season. As previously mentioned this tends to be somewhere like Spa Francorchamps, Zandvoort or Zolder, to name just a few possibilities, but testing beforehand can be limited. Unlike the UK-based track days, it's not as easy to pop by one evening for a few laps, just to quickly learn the circuit. Finding a track day company who visits some of the core European circuits is extremely useful, as you can imagine, as this could be the track experience you are missing ahead of your race. Most track day companies will plan at least one European adventure a year, with Spa Francorchamps being the most popular choice, and usually top of the list. Failing that, if you are unable to visit the circuit prior to racing there, this is where race simulators become even more useful. We will discuss race simulators in Chapter 5.

European track days can vary to that of UK events in terms of rules, and this largely depends on who you book with. If you are using your usual track day provider that you have become accustomed to for booking within the UK, it will more than likely implement the same rules for a European track day as it does for a day at Donington Park, for example. However, if you book with a company that is local to the circuit, you may find the rules differ quite a bit to what you are used to. Although you will find out more during your briefing, it is always worth familiarising yourself with any rules and regulations before booking, just to make sure the day suits you and your car.

Drawing on my own experiences of working for a track day organiser, something that I was involved in for the best part of a decade, the rules we used on our UK-based track days were exactly the same as those implemented on our European days. With three regular trips to Spa Francorchamps every year, plus at least one other, longer European track day excursion, meant we were well versed in the ways the European circuits would operate. However, implementing our regular policies, such as rules specific to overtaking, meant our customers knew exactly what to expect from our days, regardless of the circuit or country. One of the strangest things to get used to was seeing dogs at the circuit when at Spa. Animals are strictly prohibited from circuits in the UK; however, this restriction does not apply to European venues. Seeing a Labrador trotting down the pit lane at Spa will still be one of the strangest things I have seen at a circuit, and I've witnessed some strange things. On mentioning this, if you are a regular attendee to race meetings you will likely already know, but please don't try and bring your dog to one of your race meetings.

Flag signals

Regardless of whether you attend a track day in the UK or Europe, you are a car racer or a karter, communication between officials and you, the driver, is exactly the same. Motorsport uses a universal language, and it is one you will need to get used to fairly quickly. I mentioned flag signals very briefly during

Chapter 1, when discussing ARDS and ARKS licences. One of the points you need to learn in order to pass your written examination is flag signals. This is the way in which marshals and officials will communicate with you when you are on-circuit: whether it is a track day, a test day or a race meeting, flag signals remain the same. Some circuits also use a light system, meaning instead of a waved yellow flag at the scene of an incident, you may see flashing yellow lights.

Although you should know your flag signals if you have successfully passed your ARDS or ARKS test, you will also be reminded of them during each track day briefing that you attend, whether this is an online process or in person at the venue. Flag signals are extremely important and must be adhered to. I will now explain each of the signals and where you can expect to see them on a track day. The flags listed below are only specific to track days, some flags are more specific to race meetings, and as such can be found in Chapter 4: 'What to be aware of.'

Flag signal	What it means	Where you will see it
Green flag	Signals that the circuit is clear and open	At the pit exit and at marshal posts around the circuit
Yellow flag	Slow down (to 60-70% of your normal speed) as there is an incident or hazard ahead. No overtaking	At marshal posts around the circuit
Waved yellow flag	Follow instructions mentioned under Yellow flag above; however, a waved yellow flag indicates the hazard is directly ahead. This could include a car off-circuit that is being recovered, or debris on track	At marshal posts around the circuit
Red flag	No overtaking, slow your pace and return to the pit lane. Do not suddenly stop on-circuit at the sight of a red flag	At marshal posts around the circuit and pit exit
Blue flag	Very rarely used on track days. The blue flag is to let you know there is a faster car coming through. It reminds drivers to look in their mirrors, as you could be impeding the car behind you. Pull to one side at the safest opportunity to allow the car to pass safely	At marshal posts around the circuit and pit exit *(continues overleaf)*

Flag signal	What it means	Where you will see it
Black flag	The black flag indicates there is something wrong with you or your car specifically. The official waving this will also point directly at you. If you see this, move off the racing line and return to the pits immediately to speak to a member of staff or the pit lane marshal, do not hide away in your garage. The issue could be to do with noise, your driving or there could be something wrong with your car that you are not aware of, which can be dangerous	From the pit wall. The pit lane marshal will wave this at you from their position on the pit wall or near the pit exit
Black and white diagonal flag	Driving standard or track limits. You will be shown this flag if your standard of driving has fallen below an acceptable level, for example, if you are repeatedly driving beyond the edges of the track. Some circuits will impose a penalty if you are a repeat offender, this may mean missing part of your day	From the pit wall. The pit lane marshal will wave this at you from their position on the pit wall or near the pit exit
Red and yellow striped flag	This flag alerts you to something on the circuit, such as fluid or debris. It could be localised at one particular corner, or, in the case of fluid, it could be spread around the circuit. Proceed with caution	At the marshal post nearest to the fluid or debris, or at each post around the circuit if it has spread
Chequered flag	To signal the end of the session	From the pit wall

Sample schedule

Your typical track day schedule under normal circumstances will look something like the timetable shown opposite; however, in order to comply with safety regulations following the Covid19 pandemic, all organisations have since swapped to an online sign-on and briefing system in order to minimise person-to-person contact; you will complete this prior to attending your track day. This may well be a procedure that is here to stay, or we may revert back to the 'old' system, we will have to wait and see. A typical schedule will look like this:

08:00 – Sign on
08:30 – Safety briefing
09:00 – Sighting laps (led by an instructor)
09:30 – Open pit lane
12:30-13:30 – Lunch break
13:30-17:00 – Afternoon session, with the day ending at 5pm

Sighting laps are in place to allow those who are new to the circuit a few laps to figure out the layout at a steadier pace. One of the instructors who works for the track day organiser will lead the way around the sighting laps, with drivers following behind in a line. If the car you have booked to take on the track day is not ready to go, or not suitable for sighting laps, you can take your road car in its place.

Although the pace of the sighting laps is significantly slower than what you can expect throughout the track day, helmets are still a necessity. The only vehicle permitted to take more than two people will usually be the instructor car at the head of the train, but this will be another element that will differ from company to company. If you do take a different vehicle on-circuit for the sighting laps, please be sensible, you wouldn't believe the number of times I have seen someone attempt to take a motorhome on track. A word of warning, you won't usually make it out of the pit lane.

Sighting laps will often differ from circuit to circuit as well. For example, some circuits are happy that if a driver has been to the circuit before they won't enforce sighting laps on them, whereas others will insist all drivers must complete them.

Just be aware that only two people are permitted per car, no rear passengers are allowed, and all drivers and passengers must wear helmets. This is a good time to mention that your passenger will also need to sign on. Passengers usually have to be at least 16 years old, but check with your track day provider. Some companies charge a small fee for a passenger to sign on, again related to insurance requirements, whereas others allow them to sign on for free. All drivers and passengers must be signed on prior to going on-circuit, even for the sighting laps. To show you have signed on you will each receive a wristband. As a driver you will have two different coloured wristbands, one to say you have signed on as a driver and one to say you have successfully completed your safety briefing. A passenger will be given a different coloured wristband to show they too have signed on, but the different colour will signal to pitlane officials that they are not permitted to drive.

As you exit the pitlane, you will need to raise your arm to the official standing at the pit exit, to show you are wearing the correct wristbands. This must be done each time, so please bear with the officials whilst they check. As someone who has done this job many, many times, it can be difficult to see until you get closer, especially when the sun is shining on your windscreen, it renders you invisible, so please try to be patient and cooperative. When you receive your wristband, you will also be given a small sticker to affix to your car, which should go somewhere on the front of the car so officials at the pit exit know your car is permitted on track. Don't worry too much about this for the sighting laps, especially if you using a different car to the one you have booked.

The majority of track days tend to follow the open pit lane format, whereas test days are usually split into sessions. Open pit lane is always a better option, as it allows for more track time. Open pit lane basically means you can go on and off track as much as you like during the day, except for lunch time. The track will close during the lunch break, usually for one hour. This may be shortened to half an hour on winter track days to allow for maximum track time on what will probably be a shorter day than normal.

Track day rules and regulations

As with anything track based, there are specific rules you need to abide by during your track day, to ensure the safety of you and others around you when you're on-circuit. At the beginning of the day you would normally attend a safety briefing led by the Chief Instructor running the event; however, this is now something you will complete virtually before the day, under new Covid19 restrictions. You also need to ensure your car is fit for purpose before booking the event, for example if it is a race car running on slick tyres, it needs to have the correct safety equipment installed, such as a roll cage. If it is a road car, you need to make sure it has a valid MOT. Your car will not go through a scrutineering process for a track day, as it would for a race meeting, but safety is still paramount, for yourself and others on-circuit. Any issues with your car may be spotted by marshals whilst you are out on-circuit or by staff and officials in the pit lane, so it is best to ensure you are prepared. Track day insurance is not essential, but it is at your own risk should you choose not to have it, and although track day rules are in place to ensure it is a non-contact activity, whether that is with other cars or a barrier, incidents do happen.

When on-circuit the following rules* must be adhered to by all drivers and passengers:

➤ Helmets must be worn at all times (you don't need to wear your full race kit)
➤ Maximum of two people per car, no rear passengers
➤ Arms and legs must be covered, particularly in an open top car
➤ If you're in a tin top car, windows must be closed
➤ No loose objects in the car, even so much as a bottle of water – any loose objects, regardless of size can become a missile in the event of an incident

> No handheld cameras, including mobile phones. All cameras must be securely clamped to the car
> No passengers under the age of 16 years (this may differ between different companies)
> Overtaking by consent and on the left only

*This tends to be a standard set of rules, put in place by the Association of Track Day Organisers (ATDO) and implemented by all track day companies, but it is always worth checking directly with the company you have booked with, in case anything differs. Some organisers may not enforce overtaking rules, for instance.

Another thing to consider before booking a track day, briefly referred to at the beginning of this chapter, is noise. Do you know how noisy your car is? All circuits have strict noise restrictions in place, particularly for track days, and some are more strict than others. Although allowances are made for race meetings, multiple mid-week track days can often threaten the circuit's ability to run events, and some circuits are more badly affected by restrictions than others. Circuits such as Mallory Park and Croft suffer greatly with noise issues. It may seem like some circuits are surrounded by countryside, without a village in sight, but noise carries, and sadly it is something all circuits have to account for. The noise limit for a circuit or track day is usually determined by the local council, to ensure nearby residents are not disturbed, therefore the circuit is bound by these regulations to ensure they can continue to operate effectively. It is especially important that your car complies with the noise limit set by the circuit, otherwise it will be a very short and expensive day for you.

At most circuits, prior to going out on-circuit, whether that's for sighting laps or as open pit lane starts, you will need to pass a static noise test. There is usually an area in the paddock set up for noise testing. When it's your turn, you will pull up to the official carrying out the test, they will ask you to give them three quarters of your normal revs and hold it for a moment whilst they record a reading. Once passed the noise monitor will affix another small sticker to the front of your car, to let pit lane officials know that your car is allowed on-circuit. It is worth getting used to this method, as your race car will need to be noise tested at race meetings, prior to your first practice or qualifying session.

Noise control is out of the hands of the circuit staff, and although they will try and help you as much as possible, if you are caught out by the noise metre you will only have a limited number of chances to rectify this. If you are worried about the noise level of your car, have a look for unsilenced track days, where noise restrictions are removed for the day. Unsilenced events only operate on a limited number of days throughout the year and at certain circuits, Donington Park being one of them.

Track day clothing

With regard to track day clothing, you are best advised to wear something comfortable. When you take part in your first track days, you will likely want to wear your own clothing, after all, your first steps on-circuit are all about learning the ropes and building confidence. In terms of footwear, you may be inclined to wear your normal trainers for a track day; this is acceptable, but if you have already purchased, or started to gather your race kit, I would recommend wearing your race boots, even though it is not a race setting. Race boots tend to be narrow and thin soled, to help ensure maximum pedal control, plus it helps to make sure you are comfortable with your footwear whilst behind the wheel.

Once you get more comfortable with your car and with being on-circuit, you may want to wear your full race kit. Although your full race kit is not essential for a track day, it is a good opportunity to make sure you are comfortable in everything from your helmet and HANS device to your race suit, boots and gloves, and also your wrist restraints if you are racing in an open top car. The main item in your kit bag to get used to will be your HANS device. If you are used to driving a car on the road, driving with a helmet on will be a new experience, as your vision will be slightly more distorted than usual. Although you still have wing mirrors and a rear-view mirror, your rear-view mirror is often not the most helpful thing in a race car, depending on the sort of mirror you have. Some race cars will use a lightweight mirror that may be rather flimsy, so once you start racing around a circuit at 100 plus miles per hour, the vibration from the car renders it somewhat useless. Once you feel comfortable driving on-circuit, definitely make sure you do a track day with your full race kit on when you can, that way when you're sitting on the grid for your first race, you will feel more comfortable and able to concentrate on the race ahead.

Although a lot of people on a track day will be attending as a track day enthusiast, rather than using it as racing driver training, you won't stand out wearing your race kit. There will undoubtedly be other racing drivers on a test day, and you will soon notice that those who are there in a race capacity, with racing car in tow, will more than likely be wearing their full race kit. It's also a very good habit to get into with regard to safety.

Track day companies

As mentioned, there are a number of respected track day companies you can book with in the UK, each offering a slightly different experience, and suiting different budgets. Each company will offer the basics, the ability to take your own road or race car on some of the best circuits the UK has to offer. I have divulged the basics for each of the main track day organisers below, but again, this is where a bit of research comes in handy, as some will offer a little something extra, such as professional instruction or car hire. Some companies also offer novice-specific track days, something worth investigating further. A novice track day is not a regularly run event, but they are available with a bit of digging. Each track day organiser listed below will usually offer open pit-lane events, giving you ample time on-circuit throughout the day.

- **MSVT**

The track day arm of MotorSport Vision, MSVT (MSV Trackdays) organises car track days at each of the MSV circuits. Made to suit all levels of driver ability, MSVT events are very well policed, making it a suitable day for novice drivers, as well as those with more circuit experience.

- **Circuit Days**

A company that has been in existence for many years, Circuit Days offers a number of dates across the UK, as well as some European track day and road trip events. Also known for well-organised events, Circuit Days posts competitive rates for both day and evening sessions.

- **RMA**

One of the longer standing track day companies, RMA organises events both in the UK and Europe, with Donington Park, Silverstone, Brands Hatch, Oulton Park and Cadwell Park among some of its more regular destinations. Ideal for more knowledgeable track day goers, RMA days tend to be priced slightly higher, and aimed at those with more experience.

- **Javelin**

Now with more than two decades of track day organisation behind it, Javelin has been around for a long time. Offering budget friendly and cost-effective track days at circuits across the UK, you should be able to find something that suits your ability. Javelin days tend to be busier than some of the more premium track days, but always worth investigating.

- **GoldTrack**

One of the more premium track day experiences, GoldTrack offers well-organised days at some of the most popular circuits in the UK, such as Brands Hatch, Donington Park and Silverstone, as well as a number of European excursions.

- **Want2Race**

Established back in 2010, Want2Race was originally created to help novice drivers achieve their racing dream. After building a relationship with Ginetta some three years later, the two companies have since developed their involvement in the sport. In 2019 Want2Race progressed to the track day industry, organising track day events across the UK, alongside its racing exploits. Want2Race also offer car hire for all of its track days.

- **Open Track**
Another company with many years of track day experience behind them, Open Track offers days at all major UK venues, from Anglesey to Goodwood.

Once you find a track day organiser you favour, you will more than likely continue to book days with them. However, it is also worth having a look at the respective circuit websites as well, to see all available track day events. This is especially helpful for circuits such as Blyton Park in Lincolnshire. As Blyton Park doesn't hold race meetings, you will notice many of the main track day companies will not visit there, but organisers such as Javelin do. Although not beneficial to learn a circuit you won't be contesting in a race setting, Blyton Park can be extremely useful for securing some seat time and making sure you are comfortable in your race car. You can often expect to find days at Blyton don't get too busy; this is ideal for building your confidence and enjoying a day on-circuit.

TEST DAYS

Test days run slightly differently to track days, and they are more geared towards racing drivers. The rules will differ to that of a track day, for instance you must be a race licence holder, and overtaking can take place on either side. You will need your race licence to sign on for a test day, not your road licence. Make sure you check with the organiser before attending if you plan to bring an instructor that you would like to sit in the car with – some organisers won't allow instructors to passenger in car with you, due to insurance restrictions. You will also notice a significant difference in the cost of a test day to that of a track day, a consideration that is worth bearing in mind.

Having an instructor with you on a track or test day is massively beneficial. Depending on what you want to gain from your instruction session, it may be better to have your driver coach join you on a test day, rather than a track day. As mentioned in the track day section, it may be more convenient to have an instructor join you on a track day, as they will definitely be able to join you in car on-circuit. However, it is more beneficial to have them attend a test day with you, as they can help with data and lap times, for instance and timing is not permitted on a track day. Although having an extra person in the car may not always be the best preparation for a race, as it will change the dynamics of the car, it is useful to have an instructor sat beside you on-circuit, so they can show you the correct racing lines and braking points.

During a sessioned test day, drivers will initially head out on-circuit for their first session, to see how they find the car and circuit combination with the conditions available to them at the time. Test day sessions are usually between 20 to 30 minutes long, giving ample time to bank some good data. The downtime in-between track sessions is then spent with your driver coach, deciphering your data, analysing your lap times, looking at where you can recover more time and in turn produce quicker lap times, which is the ultimate goal. You will find that professional instructors booked for a test day will go through your data with you, whereas this doesn't usually apply to track day instructors. When booking an instructor through your track day provider, you will usually have your 20-minute session on-circuit and receive some feedback, but there will not be any data to go through or take away with you.

Although you will have access to your timing data as part of your in-car timing system (discussed in Chapter 4), some test days often utilise well known motorsport timing systems, such as Timing Solutions Limited (TSL). TSL will usually be in attendance on a Friday test day, setting up and preparing for that weekend's race meeting, and will often supply timing for the Friday test day as well, although you may need to book this in advance. This service can be useful, as you can see what sort of times the rest of your fellow competitors are recording, which gives you an idea of where you will be in terms of pace come race day.

Booking a qualified driver coach for a day on-circuit can be costly, depending on who you book, but it is a worthwhile and invaluable experience. There is no substitute for spending a day on-circuit with a qualified professional to guide you. If you find the day costly, why not share your instructor between you and a fellow racing driver? Once you start to make friends within your championship, it's likely you will book the same test and track days as one another. This is the ideal opportunity to share a day of coaching.

Always double-check the sort of test day you are booking: some days run as open pit lane, although the majority of test days will be split into sessions to allow for different cars to run separately. Sessioned days often allow for each group to have four sessions, but this all depends on the organiser.

The Friday, or sometimes Thursday and Friday before a race meeting is usually dedicated to test days. If you plan to complete the Friday test day prior to your race meeting, I recommend you book this as early as possible. As with track days, only so many places are available, and they tend to fill rather quickly.

More often than not, the Friday test day of your race weekend will be organised through the circuit you are competing at, meaning you will book the day directly with the circuit, rather than your racing club. All track and test days can be viewed and booked on the respective circuit's website, so it is always best to have a look there first. As with track days, dates will begin to appear towards the beginning of the year, I can't stress enough just how vital it is to book as early as possible. This has been particularly important since the start of Covid19, as due to a lack of track time during lockdown periods, available track and test days have been selling out within a matter of hours in some cases.

When planning for your track or test days, don't forget to consider your consumables, such as fuel. Fuel is usually available on site at the circuit, but be prepared to spend a lot more than you would at your local fuel station. The best solution, to save some money, is to invest in some jerry cans, you'll need these for race meetings anyway, and either fill them up prior to getting to the circuit, or nip out during the day to the nearest fuel station. It may be worth having a look before arriving at the circuit, to check how far away the nearest off-site fuel station is. You don't want to be driving miles and losing part of your day, although if you can arrive at the circuit with enough fuel for half a day, you can usually use the lunch break to go and stock up, without losing part of your track time.

You will have seen the table earlier in this section regarding flag signals. The same flags will be used on a test day as on a track day. Track days and test days tend to use the red flag more than other track activity, rather than carry out a live recovery. A live recovery is essentially when the recovery truck goes out on-circuit to recover a stricken car whilst the circuit is still live, under a yellow flag situation, rather than a red flag. Again, those drivers in particular who are booked on a test day should be familiar with the Motorsport UK flag signals, as this is something they had to know to gain their race licence.

CHAPTER 4

RACE MEETINGS

So, you are armed with your ARKS or ARDS licence, you have found the right kart or car, tested it to within an inch of its life, joined your racing club and registered for your chosen championship or series, and are kitted out from head to toe in the latest safety equipment. What's next? Now it really gets serious, it's time to book some race meetings. This first section focuses on kart race meetings, with the subsequent section dedicated to car racing. I will also discuss additional equipment you will need, relating more to races, such as timing equipment and data logging.

BOOKING YOUR FIRST KART RACE MEETING

Kart race meetings can be booked through your kart club or championship, and is usually an online process. For those without online access, you can request race entry forms from your club secretary; complete these and send back to the competition secretary of your club. In order to book, you must first be registered with your club and respective championship; again, you will be able to do this through your main club contacts.

Depending on the event, the organising club could have anything from 70 to 200 drivers to organise, as well as between seven and 11 classes. Many clubs will hold a practice day prior to the event, usually on the first day of the event, for instance, a Saturday morning. The practice session is usually the first track action for drivers during a race meeting, giving a chance to sample the circuit and test the conditions before heading into qualifying. More often than not, the morning practice session will be a costed event, with prices varying depending on the event, but this is usually something you will book in advance, so you will know how much to factor into your racing budget for the weekend. Some clubs will only allow those entered in that specific race meeting to enter the practice day, although others will open up the session to all those with a kart that fits the event regulations.

Many organisations involved in the karting industry use the Alpha Timing system for race entry bookings and management, and club administrative tasks, as well as live event timing. This system allows the organising clubs and drivers to manage bookings, with drivers also able to easily make secure payments online. As many clubs use the same management system, this makes things that bit easier for you if you race with different clubs, as you are already familiar with the online system.

Karting transponders

Another cost associated with your race meetings, and something that will need to be processed during the booking system, is a transponder. You will need to register your transponder number with your organising club, this can be found on the actual transponder itself. It is an essential piece of equipment, as it enables the event's timing system to track your movements, lap times and results around the circuit during practice, qualifying sessions, and your competitive heats and finals. In order for the transponder to work effectively, you will need to affix it to the rear of your kart seat. It will then send a signal to a loop buried in the circuit, usually situated at the start/finish line. There will also be other loops around the circuit that will enable the timing system to measure sector times during each lap. You can either hire a transponder or buy one outright. If you are hiring a transponder, you will need to do this ahead of each race event, an additional cost you will need to allow for each time.

If you would prefer to purchase, there are two companies from whom you can buy your transponder, one is called MYLAPS, which specialises in all manner of automated timing for a variety of sports, the other is TAG-Heuer. Although I say you are buying a transponder, you are effectively purchasing a subscription that includes the actual transponder you attach to your kart.

If you choose MYLAPS, there are two types of transponder you can choose from, both of which are specific to karting. One is the X2 transponder, powered directly from your car's battery, the other is the newer TR2 transponder, which is a rechargeable device.

In terms of live timing, there are different systems used in kart racing that work in conjunction with the different transponder. The SuperSports system is the original timing system used by the majority of kart clubs; however, it is now often surpassed by newer systems. SuperSports tends to use the MYLAPS transponders. Apex software is marketed in the UK by TAG-Heuer, and is used together with the TAG Heuer transponders. The final system, and one that is now used by a large number of kart clubs, is Alpha Timing. This system can be used with both MYLAPS and TAG-Heuer transponders. If you want to check your results after an event, which of course you will, you can do this using the following websites:

➤ Motorsport Timing UK – www.motorsport-timing.co.uk

This timing system has been developed for UK kart circuits, using the TAG Heuer transponder

> Alpha Timing – www.results.alphatiming.co.uk

As previously mentioned, there are two types of transponder available through MYLAPS, the X2 transponder and the TR2. The X2 is compatible with all MYLAPS timing systems. The standard device comes as a rechargeable model, or as a direct power upgrade, which can be permanently charged by your kart's battery. Each model has the option to also choose a one-year, two-year or five-year subscription. To purchase this device, the associated costs are as follows:

> Standard transponder (no upgrade) with.one-year subscription – approximately £73
> Standard transponder (no upgrade) with two-year subscription – approximately £111
> Standard transponder (no upgrade) with five-year subscription – approximately £189
> Direct power upgrade transponder with one-year subscription – approximately £120
> Direct power upgrade transponder with two-year subscription – approximately £163
> Direct power upgrade transponder with five-year subscription – approximately £250

The TR2 transponder is the newest on the market. With an unlimited warranty during active subscriptions, this transponder is also rechargeable. As with the X2, you can select either a one-, two- or five-year subscription:

> TR2 transponder with one-year subscription – approximately £77
> TR2 transponder with two-year subscription – approximately £111
> TR2 transponder with five-year subscription – approximately £198
> TR2 Go Transponder (no subscription – approximately £345

Once your initial subscription period has come to an end with either transponder you can renew your payment.

With regard to the TAG-Heuer transponder, the TAG-Heuer Protime LS transponder is designed specifically for kart racing. Once fully charged, the power will last for several months, usually with just one charge needed per year to ensure it maintains full working order. The cost for this transponder differs depending on where you purchase it, but the price tends to start around the £200 mark.

The clubs using the Alpha Timing system include:

> ➤ Camberley Kart Club (Blackbushe circuit)
> ➤ Cheshire Kart Club (Hooton Park circuit)
> ➤ Clay Pigeon
> ➤ Dragon Kart Club (Glan y Gors circuit)
> ➤ Dunkeswell Kart Club
> ➤ Forest Edge Kart Club
> ➤ Cumbria Kart Club (Rowrah circuit)
> ➤ Manchester and Buxton Kart Club (Three Sisters circuit)
> ➤ Shenington Kart Club
> ➤ NatSKA
> ➤ Whilton Mill
> ➤ West of Scotland Kart Club (Larkhall circuit)

The clubs who use the TAG-Heuer timing system include:

> ➤ Hunts Kart Club (Kimbolton circuit)
> ➤ Trent Valley Kart Club (PF International)

Now you have booked your race meeting, you have your transponder, you have your list of essential equipment ready to pack, and you know exactly where to look to check your results. You are all set for your first race meeting.

Onboard cameras and footage

A camera is quite often a mandatory piece of equipment for all drivers, whether you are involved in karting or car racing. Although cameras are generally affixed to karts to assist with any judicial issues, it is often used as a driver training tool. Whether you make use of a qualified driver coach, or just review your race data yourself, a camera can be a useful tool for helping to improve your on-track performance.

Your organising club will likely specify whether you need to have a camera onboard, and also where it needs to be attached. For karts with forward facing cameras, Motorsport UK regulations state that the image shown on the camera must be shown from a driver's eye view, as well as displaying the circuit with a field of vision of approximately 100 degrees. Kart drivers will need to ensure that both front wheels are shown on their footage, and may also be required to affix rear facing cameras for official purposes, but this will be at the discretion of your specific supplementary regulations.

If you wish to attach cameras to other parts of your kart, this may be allowed, but it will need approval from the chief scrutineer, to ensure they are attached in a safe place and manner. Regardless of where a camera is fitted, it will need to be attached with a suitable mechanism that can withstand the vibrations and stress associated with high speeds when you are on-circuit. You should also ensure external cameras are attached with a secondary fitting, for example, a suction mount alone will not be suitable, it will need to be tethered as well.

Kart race meeting procedure

Normally, upon arrival at the circuit on race day, the first port of call would be sign on. However, following the changes in 2020 due to the pandemic, in order to minimise contact between people, many race meeting admin tasks changed to an online process. This is a universal procedure that has been set out by Motorsport UK. Now with a successful online system in place, this is likely to be something that is here to stay, for the time being at least. However, some clubs may opt to return to previous sign-on methods.

In order to successfully sign on, you will need to produce your race licence, which must be signed and in date, of course. For those who are under 18 years of age, you will need a parent or guardian to not only attend each event with you, but to also countersign any forms you need to fill in. Your parent or guardian will also need a PG Entrant Licence; however, for those who are under the age of 18 years old and just about to get your first karting race licence, this is included with your Go Karting pack and costs an additional £25. After that you will need to apply for an Entrant Licence through Motorsport UK. This licence normally costs £195 and is valid for karting in the UK.

Prior to Covid19, following sign-on you would then be asked to go see the scrutineering team. The scrutineers would check your race kit and kart, to make sure everything is legal, safe and in date, where applicable. However, in 2020, this was another process that was largely changed to an online system. When completing the online sign-on process, you will also be required to complete a self-declaration, which includes acknowledging your race kit. This effectively acts as your scrutineering, although some drivers may be called for scrutineering in person at the circuit, this will be a random selection. You may also have to attend a mandatory drivers' briefing that will inform you of any important information specific to the event. Once you have passed all checks and you are signed on, you are good to go.

Following practice, the real action begins. Normally, again depending on the club and the type of event, each driver will contest two or three heats and a final. During the heats, grid positions are allocated to drivers from the club officials. To make it a fair competition, drivers who have been at the head of the grid for the first heat will likely be allocated a spot towards the rear of the grid for the second heat. However, if you are a novice driver, you will more than likely start at the back of the grid at first. A novice driver will be easy to spot, for those who are more experienced. Whilst novice drivers in car racing will sport a square yellow sticker with a black cross on it, novice karters are required to display black number boards with white numbers, to alert other drivers.

As you approach the final, your grid position is determined by the points you are awarded during the heats. So, the more competitive you can be during the heats, it will stand you in good stead for the final. As an alternative, some organisations may run a timed qualifying session, with each driver competing for their grid position. Positions will then be determined in order of fastest time. Those that finish in the first three of four positions in each class can also look forward to receiving some silverware, a nice reward for your efforts during the day.

What to be aware of – karting

One of the most important things to be aware of when karting is the communication between you and the officials. I discussed flag signals and their importance in Chapter 3; however, flag signals in kart racing differ ever so slightly to that of track days and car racing. Track days use only a few flags to communicate with drivers on-circuit, although there are more that are commonly used in racing that all drivers need to understand.

Bearing in mind, once you pass your ARKS licence you should be fluent in the way of flag signals, as you will need to know what each of them mean as part of your written examination. With that in mind, here is a run through of each of the flags used in karting. Some kart circuits may also use a lights system to communicate with you, to reflect the flags commonly used, for instance instead of a waved yellow flag, this may be replaced with a flashing yellow light.

Flag signal	What it means	Where you will see it
Green flag	Signals that the circuit is clear and open. The green flag will also be used to indicate to the start of the formation lap before the start of a race	At all marshal posts around the circuit
Stationary yellow flag	Slow down (to 60-70% of your normal speed) to ensure you have complete control of your vehicle, as there is an incident or hazard ahead. No overtaking	At marshal posts around the circuit
Waved yellow flag	Follow instructions mentioned under Yellow Flag above; however, a waved yellow flag indicates more danger as the hazard is directly ahead. Be prepared to deviate from your normal racing line to avoid any hazards	At the marshal posts nearest to where the incident or hazard is on-circuit

Flag signal	What it means	Where you will see it
Red flag	No overtaking, slow your pace and return to the pit lane or start line. Do not suddenly stop on-circuit at the sight of a red flag. Watch out for officials as you approach the pit lane or starting grid, as they may be on-circuit to direct you	At all marshal posts around the circuit
Blue flag	The blue flag is to let you know there is a faster car coming through. It reminds drivers to look in their mirrors, as you could be impeding the car behind you. Pull to one side at the safest opportunity to allow the car to pass safely. In a race situation you are likely to be shown the blue flag if you are about to be lapped	At the relevant marshal posts around the circuit
Black flag	The black flag indicates that you have done something wrong. You must return to the pit lane within one lap of seeing the black flag and report to the Clerk of the Course. A penalty of exclusion may be enforced	From the pit wall. The pit lane marshal will wave this at you from their position on the pit wall, usually together with a pit board displaying your racing number
Black and white diagonal flag	Driving standard or track limits. You will be shown this flag if your standard of driving has fallen below acceptable. For example, if you are repeatedly driving beyond the edges of the track. You will be shown this a certain number of times before being shown the black flag, so it is imperative you pay attention	From the pit wall. The pit lane marshal will wave this at you from their position on the pit wall near the pit exit
Red and yellow striped flag	This flag alerts you to something on the circuit, such as fluid or debris. It could be localised at one particular corner or, in the case of fluid, it could be spread around the circuit. Proceed with caution	At the marshal post nearest to the fluid or debris, or at each post around the circuit if it has spread

(continues overleaf)

Flag signal	What it means	Where you will see it
Chequered flag	To signal the end of the session or race	From the pit wall
Union Jack	This is used to start a race in the absence of lights. For rolling starts you will start when the flag is raised, for standing starts you will start as the flag drops	At the start line
Green flag with yellow lines	False start. Slow down and reform the grid. Continue on another formation lap, remain in grid order and proceed at the speed set by the pole sitter	At the start line
Black flag with orange circle	To notify the driver there is an issue such as a mechanical failure or fire that they may not be aware of. This could also include loose bodywork. Return to the pits to have the issue rectified	From the pit wall
Yellow and black chequered flag	Immediately slow down and form up behind the leader, no overtaking until a green flag is shown at the start line. The lead kart will dictate the pace, similar to a formation lap at the start of a race	From the pit wall
White flag	There is a slow moving vehicle on-circuit. This could be a slow moving kart or a service vehicle, such as recovery or ambulance	At marshal posts around the circuit

BOOKING YOUR FIRST CAR RACE MEETING

Although the different race clubs will vary in many operational ways, a lot of them tend to use the same booking system, just to help make things as simple as possible. One system, used by the 750 Motor Club, BARC, and until recently, the BRSCC, is called RevUp. During this chapter we will explain more about the booking process, what happens in the build up to your event and also what to do during your first race meeting.

As with so many things, the race meeting booking process is an online activity, although paper entry forms are readily available upon request, for those who prefer or for those without online access. One of the benefits of using the online system means you can easily manage your calendar, with everything easily accessible and in one place, and it helps to keep tabs on which events you have booked and paid for. Although many of the race clubs use the same booking system, if you race with different clubs, you will have a different login for each one. So, for instance, if you decide to do some races with the 750 Motor Club and some with the BARC, you won't be able to see all races for both clubs in one place, you will need to login from the respective club's website.

You may have made the decision to start racing part way through the year, with a view to joining the grid next year. The race calendar for the following season will likely be released during the last few months of the year, giving you time to plan and prepare your season. Just be aware, all dates tend to be provisional when first released, race dates can, and often do, change. If your plan is to attend every race meeting, it is best to book each round at the start of the season, if your club allows. At this point, familiarise yourself with your club's booking system and payment policy, so you are prepared once race entries open.

As an example, let's run through the procedure with the 750 Motor Club. Membership can be purchased at any time, not just at the start of the season, and as mentioned in Chapter 2, membership with 750MC is valid for 12 months from date of purchase, not January to December. So, you have purchased your club membership and now you're eagerly awaiting the next step. With regard to 750MC, registrations for your respective championship or series will usually open towards the end of January, with race entries open a further two weeks after that. You have registered and received details via email for logging into the online system. Once race entries open, when you log in to the online race portal you will see all available dates for the championship(s) you have registered for, you can then book as many or as few as you wish. Although you may have booked for a full season, you won't be out of pocket right away. Payment for each event is due 21 days prior to that event, so you can pay as you go, helping to manage budget restraints. Just remember this is the payment policy for 750MC, each club will differ when it comes to race payments.

As with a track or test day, entry numbers will be restricted for race meetings. Grid capacity is limited and differs from circuit to circuit. Smaller circuits, such as Cadwell Park will have a lower grid capacity than that of the Silverstone GP circuit, for instance. Some race meetings will always prove to be more popular than others, with the likes of Donington Park and Brands Hatch usually proving to be two of the most popular 'bucket list' circuits, so it is best to make sure you are booked in nice and early, rather than having to rely on withdrawals in the eleventh hour. If you do end up on a reserve list for a race, don't be too disheartened. I have seen championships with more than 20 competitors on a reserve list, all of whom manage to get a spot on the grid come race day. It really does happen. Some drivers will book every event at the start of the year; however, as the season progresses cars become damaged or suffer mechanical failures, and drivers may have work and family commitments to contend with, so withdrawals from a race meeting are common.

Car racing transponders

I touched on the topic of transponders very briefly at the beginning of Chapter 1, and now is the time to discuss this in more detail. All competitors must have a transponder attached to their race car. This is purely for race meetings and doesn't relate to track days. The transponder allows the events timing system to track you on-circuit, record your lap times and your qualifying or race position, so it is rather important. If your transponder is not fitted correctly you will often see the note 'transponder (or Tx) not working' next to your name on the timing results. In this case, you will need to adjust your transponder position.

There are two options when it comes to using a transponder, you can either buy your own or hire one. In the case of 750MC, you can hire a transponder directly from the Club at a cost of £30 per race meeting. 750MC uses a different timing system to other clubs, and so operates in a slightly different way when it comes to transponders. The timing system used by 750MC is called The Results Live (www.theresultslive.co.uk), whereas the majority of other clubs and organisations use Timing Solutions Ltd (more commonly referred to as TSL). TSL is the most popular timing system used in UK motorsport and more universally known by competitors. All manner of clubs and championships use the TSL system, from club level to more prominent events, such as the British GT Championship, and even events further afield, such as some Formula One testing, and international GT events. All other clubs, aside from 750MC, will use TSL and it is very user friendly. Information supplied on the online system includes lap times for all race weekend sessions, from free practice and qualifying to races. It will show positions for each driver, individual sector and lap times for each driver, and even class winners and fastest lap holders in the race results. For drivers competing in events that use the TSL system, you can hire a transponder directly from them. Single event transponder hire for events from TSL Timing is also £30 per event. In both cases you will need to hire your transponder beforehand and collect it from race admin at the event.

If you would prefer to buy a transponder, this is another cost to factor into your racing budget. One of the bonus points of buying a transponder is that it is one less thing to remember to sort out before a race meeting, you always have it attached to your car and ready to go. You will need to make sure your organising club has your transponder number before your first event, to ensure it can be passed to the timing company prior to the race meeting. You can find your transponder number on the front of the device.

When attaching the transponder to your car, make sure you affix it in the correct place. It needs to sit in the front of your car, usually as far forward as possible, but do double-check with your championship's supplementary regulations, as some championships may stipulate exactly where the transponder needs to be attached. Placing the device as far forward as possible enables the timing beacons set up at the circuit to register your car as it passes each lap in order to record sector and full lap times. Make sure you attach it securely, using your trusty cable ties.

As mentioned above, under 'Booking your first kart race meeting', transponders for car racing can also be purchased directly from MYLAPS, or from TSL. If you missed the introduction in the karting section, MYLAPS specialises in automated sport timing. Whether you buy your device from MYLAPS directly or from TSL, there are two transponders to choose from. One is the X2 transponder that comes as either the standard rechargeable option (no upgrade) or it can be permanently powered directly from your car's battery (the direct power upgrade option). This transponder also requires a subscription, with the price including the hardware as well as subscription for either one year, two years or five years. When you first receive your transponder, you will need to activate it by connecting it to a computer. The features of the X2 transponder include:

> Unlimited warranty during your active subscription
> Compatibility with all MYLAPS timing systems
> Easy and free online access to all of your practice and race results on the Speedhive app and website
> Improved battery charging

Upon purchasing your device, you will receive your X2 transponder, a transponder holder, an X2 RaceKey, which helps to manage your subscription and also charge your device, as well as a RaceKey holder. For those who opt for the upgrade option, you will also receive a USB 12V cable and CAN cable to use with your device. To purchase the X2 transponder directly from MYLAPS you would be looking at the following costs (please bear in mind MYLAPS is a European company so the prices below have been converted to pounds sterling, so conversion rates may differ):

> Standard, no upgrade device with one year subscription: approximately £120
> Standard, no upgrade device with two years subscription: approximately £163
> Standard, no upgrade device with five years subscription: approximately £284
> Direct power upgrade device with one year subscription: approximately £163
> Direct power upgrade device with two years subscription: approximately £224

➤ Direct power upgrade device with five years subscription: approximately £353

The second option is the TR2 transponder, a newer, innovative device that works in the same way as the X2, and includes many of the same elements, but with a few additional features. Together with your transponder, you will also receive a TR2 charge cradle, including a USB micro cable, as well as transponder holder. The prices for the TR2 transponder directly from MYLAPS, are as follows:

➤ Transponder including one year subscription: approximately £128
➤ Transponder including two years subscription: approximately £172
➤ Transponder including five years subscription: approximately £302
➤ TR2 Go Transponder (no subscription): approximately £475

Both the X2 and TR2 transponders can also be purchased from TSL, although prices will differ.

In-car cameras and data logging
Another essential item to make sure you have in place prior to your first race meeting is a camera. Many championships and series will stipulate in the respective regulations if a camera is required, and if so they will also confirm the exact required position. More often than not, each car needs to have at least one piece of recording equipment attached to it in order to abide by set regulations. Many drivers have a forward-facing camera to fully enhance their race information; this helps when analysing your data. From a regulation point of view, it is also an essential piece of equipment, as it could support you in the event on being called to see the Clerk of the Course. The Clerk of the Course is one of the main officials working at a race meeting, who holds the overall responsibility for control and general conduct of the event. For those championships that state the need for a forward facing camera, the device should be affixed to the car in a position that shows a driver's eye view, so as to capture anything that could be discussed in a judicial capacity. Ideally, this view should include the steering wheel, dashboard, and a view of the circuit with a field view of approximately 100 degrees. In single-seater, or open wheel cars the front wheels should be shown in shot where possible as well. A rear facing camera may be required, but many drivers tend to fit these, to help with driving coaching.
  You will usually be called to see the Clerk of the Course if you have either caused an event, been involved in an event, or perhaps you were an onlooker and caught incident footage on your camera. Upon being called, you will usually be asked to bring your camera footage with you for the officials to

analyse and make an informed decision as to whether a driver should receive a penalty or not. Penalties range from a fine to both a fine and points on your race licence. As you progress up the motor racing ladder, this could prove very costly, in terms of your championship campaign. In championships such as the Ginetta G40 Cup for example, if you receive penalty points on your race licence, this also equates to a deduction in championship points. If you do become involved in an altercation on-circuit, you may just receive a slap on the wrist, if you're lucky, but it is worth being aware of the worst-case scenario. If you are called into a judicial meeting and do not have camera footage, this will be recorded as failing to provide camera evidence, even if it is a case of your camera failing to work and an issue with your footage downloading; this may or may not work in your favour.

The number of cameras you have, and the positioning of them, is personal preference. For example, many Caterham racers will have two cameras on their roll cage, one facing forwards and one facing backwards. Some drivers, regardless of the car they are racing, also like to have a camera pointing at their feet, so they can see their foot movements on the pedals. This can be advantageous if you are using a driver coach, as they can help adjust your foot movements and introduce new skills, such as the heel and toe manoeuvre, a technique many racing drivers often adopt.

I referred to data logging briefly in Chapter 3, when discussing instruction, but this is another important device you will need. There are many different devices to use when it comes to data logging, depending on what you want to do with the information and once again, your available budget.

RACELOGIC is the leading company in the field, with many years of experience designing and developing video-enhanced data to be used in a variety of race cars, it is an expert in data logging systems. The most popular, and extremely advanced, data logging equipment used in motorsport to come from RACELOGIC is the VBOX system. This is a product that is universally accepted as being one of the best systems on the market, with a vast majority of drivers using some form of VBOX device in their race car.

The latest, top of the range version is called the VBOX Video HD2, and it is the most sophisticated recording equipment available to racing drivers at all levels of motorsport. Included in the VBOX Video HD2 pack is two waterproof cameras, giving dual camera input with 60 frames per second. This saves you having to purchase cameras separately, as the two cameras can be used as front and rear-facing cameras in your car. The software will also include CAN Bus Input, meaning you can log up to 80 channels of vehicle CAN data, such as throttle angle, revs per minute, and brake pressure. You will also have high definition video footage and real-time graphics, allowing you to fully analyse your race footage.

The device also has the option of an OLED display, which gives you accurate real-time lap comparisons between your current and your fastest laps. Additionally, the VBOX comes with a free system that enables intuitive circuit tools analysis software.

The VBOX HD2 really is a state-of-the-art piece of equipment that most drivers will use; however, due to its advanced nature, it does have a price tag attached to reflect this. The latest piece of equipment costs £2310, including VAT. Just remember that this is the full piece of equipment, although you can purchase certain items individually, to help with budget restraints.

An alternative device is the VBOX lap timer. This is a predictive lap timing display and GPS data logger in one. It provides instant driver feedback, allowing you to analyse your lap times effectively. The display mode features include:

> Live speed
> Maximum speed
> Lap timing
> Split times and your best lap times
> Predictive lap timing

The price for this device is £738 inclusive of VAT. The VBOX lap timer is a beneficial piece of equipment; however, remember you would still need to purchase your cameras separately.

Finally, there is the Video VBOX Lite, often described as the club racer's VBOX. It includes a host of features at a more budget friendly price. Used by the majority of club level competitors, this device comprises a solid state video recorder, a GPS data-logger and real-time graphic overlay, all in one smaller box. This option is more than suitable for driver training and data analysis, whilst still being user friendly for those who are new to data logging equipment. Included with the Video VBOX Lite system is:

> GPS data logger and video recorder, incorporating graphic overlay
> One Sony HQ1 bullet camera and windscreen suction mount
> One Sony ⅓in bullet camera and windscreen mount
> Two ring clamp mounts for the hi-res main camera
> Two microphones (to use with driver coaching)
> Microphone splitter cable
> Magnetic GPS antenna
> In-car power supply cable to connect to a 12V aux supply or cigarette lighter
> 8GB SD card, featuring device software and user guide

The price for this device is £1194, including VAT.
Each of the various VBOX devices will operate with a normal SD card that

should be inserted prior to each qualifying session or race meeting. It is this SD card that you will need to take with you in the event of being called to see the Clerk of the Course.

An alternative system is the Aim Technologies device. Offering data logging equipment for car racing, motorbikes, kart racing and motocross, there is a good range of products available, but this section will of course focus on what's available for those looking at car racing.

The products available with Aim Technologies vary from a track day kit for those looking to improve their basic track driving performance, to kits specific to certain cars. Starting with the track day kit, although lap timing is not allowed on a track day, the footage you can capture with this kit will help to develop your performance on-circuit. In terms of pricing for this product, if you contact Aim Technologies directly with your personal specifications about what you want to achieve with your kit, they will supply you with a quote.

With regard to dash display systems, Aim Technologies have a number of systems available in their shop. The range of dash loggers include:

➤ The MXS 1.2
  This is the new 5in (12.7cm) dash logger, designed to display data taken from your engine control unit (ECU)
➤ The MXP Dash Logger
  The slightly bigger 6in (15.2cm) dash logger also comes with Wi-Fi, USB connectivity and a GPS module
➤ The MXG 1.2 Dash Logger
  At 7in (17.8cm) this is an extra wide dash logger. Designed specifically for motorsport, the device features a high contrast display, fully configurable by a dedicated software

The following dash loggers are an upgrade on a previous model, and is something that is popular with racing drivers worldwide:

➤ The MXS 1.2 Strada Dash Logger
➤ The MXP Strada Dash Logger
➤ The MXG 1.2 Strada Dash Logger

The products listed below are all LCD dash data loggers:

➤ The MXL2 Dash Logger
  Another product that has been designed for motorsport, this data logger comes equipped with a high contrast traditional LCD
➤ The MXm Dash Logger

Designed to allow racing drivers to easily read all of the data needed from the car and driving performance. Its compact size fits your dash perfectly

Dedicated dash systems include devices for Lotus Elise and Lotus Exige cars, as well as the Legends race cars. By browsing the Aim Technologies website, you will also see a range of data loggers that are compatible with the various dash loggers. For prices relating to all Aim Technologies products, you can contact them directly with details about what you would like to gain from your equipment, and they will provide you with a bespoke quote.

As long as you are sporting your transponder, a forward-facing camera and your lap timing data equipment, you will be okay. However, it's at this point where some drivers can become somewhat gadget-obsessed, and, as you can imagine, may increase your budget tenfold without being necessary. It's all about personal preference.

Now you are armed with the necessary equipment and setup, let's look at what actually happens during a race meeting.

Car race meeting procedure

You may be well versed in motorsport and therefore know the basics of how a race meeting operates; however, there will likely be plenty of details that you will only become aware of when you register as a competitor. Throughout this section I will discuss what to expect on race day, so you can turn up to your first race meeting feeling much more prepared.

During 2020 we witnessed a drastic change to the race meeting procedure, due to the Covid-19 pandemic. For those just beginning their motor racing journey, this 'new' way of working will be the norm, although for those used to the previous routine, it has taken some adjusting.

Although you have prepared your car and booked your race, there is still more to go through before you're sitting on the grid. As with a track or test day, you must follow a sign-on procedure. Previously, all race meeting sign-on procedures took place at the circuit, in the race admin office. The driver would have their race licence checked by the organisers in person, to ensure it was in date, sign next to their name on the form in front of them, and then be handed all relevant paperwork and information they needed ahead of the event, and away they would go.

Now, following Motorsport UK guidelines, all organising clubs have implemented an online sign-on system, to limit person-to-person contact at an event. Following a successful trial during the 2020 season, it appears as though this procedure will become a permanent fixture for race weekends, negating the need to print masses of paperwork for each event, for both the driver and organisers. It also means that as a driver, you can arrive at your event knowing you have successfully signed on, giving you one less thing to worry about. In the case of junior racing drivers, as with track days and test days, you will need a parent or guardian to countersign your declaration.

Under the new requirements, prior to your first race meeting of the year, you are required to email a photo of your race licence to the appointed person at your organising club, and this will be kept on file for the season. For most organisers you only need to send this prior to your first event; however, for others, such as MSVR, you will need to do this ahead of each event. Seven days prior to each event, you will then be able to access online sign-on via your club's online race portal. Just be aware that the 'sign-on' option may only become visible once your race entry has been paid for, especially if you are using the RevUp system, so make sure this is processed in plenty of time to avoid any unnecessary last-minute stress. The sooner you sign on the sooner you will also receive your tickets for the weekend. Again, the earlier this process is completed the better, as it reduces your list of things to remember, leaving you to focus on your race. All MSV circuits (Brands Hatch, Oulton Park, Donington Park, Snetterton, and Cadwell Park), and now Silverstone, issue e-tickets for all race meetings, although other circuits will issue a paper ticket, which will be posted to your nominated address. Tickets may only be distributed once you have paid for your event. As you can appreciate, the sooner this is processed, the easier it makes things for you. E-tickets can be scanned from your smartphone; however,, try to print them if you can to avoid any issues.

A top tip when you're ready to sign on is to make sure you have your safety equipment to hand. In place of physical scrutineering, you must complete a declaration as part of the sign-on process, to acknowledge the date of your helmet, HANS device, first extinguisher and seatbelts, for instance. Perhaps make a note of expiration dates and other details on your equipment checklist and keep it somewhere safe that you can access easily and quickly. Under 'normal' circumstances, you would have been given a scrutineering ticket upon passing any safety checks, and this would be attached to the inside of your car. However, this is something that has since become obsolete, for the time being at least.

All this may seem somewhat daunting, but after you have completed the process once it will soon become second nature. For those who don't have computer access or are unable to complete any of this process online, you can contact your organising club for a paper copy of all forms.

So, you have signed on, you've received your tickets and you're ready to race, right? This is the time to dig out your checklist and make sure you have packed everything you need. The likelihood is that someone at the circuit will have things to borrow, or as mentioned previously you could purchase replacement safety equipment and clothing either on site or nearby, but why leave it to chance. It's always best to be prepared. You don't want any last minute panic attacks.

SO, YOU WANT TO BE A RACING DRIVER?

Depending on whether you have booked a pre-race weekend test day or not will determine how much time you need to leave to travel to the circuit. If you are testing on the Friday, people generally arrive Thursday evening, to set up and make sure you have arrived in plenty of time, although you don't have to. Arriving early Friday morning is perfectly acceptable. Obviously when you plan to arrive also depends on your personal circumstances, for instance if you have work or family commitments, and whether or not you plan to stay in a hotel. Any extra nights in a hotel adds to your weekend budget, of course. If you are not testing and only racing, you can even arrive early Saturday morning, just remember you need to allow enough time to get set up and be ready in time for any scrutineering checks, should you be selected for a random spot check. Arriving at the circuit Friday evening, if you can, to drop your car off and set up anything you have with you, will be very beneficial, and it is a weight off your mind knowing you don't have much to do Saturday morning. If you are staying in a hotel, it means you can leave your car safely at the circuit and not worry about finding somewhere to park a car and trailer at your hotel.

If you have opted for a team to transport and run your car, you just need to remember to turn up, with your equipment of course; however, if you are your own support team, a highly likely scenario in your first season, as simple as it sounds, make sure you remember your toolbox. I can't stress enough the importance of gaffer tape, cable ties and blue roll during a race weekend. Add them to your essential kit list.

If you do arrive at the circuit the day before you are racing, why not spend the evening walking the circuit. You are allowed to do this once track action has finished for the day, and all officials have finished on-circuit, such as the marshals and circuit maintenance staff. This is particularly useful if this is your first visit to the circuit and you haven't had time to test or practise. It will give you an idea of where the circuit goes before seeing it for the first time in qualifying.

More often than not, track action starts from 9am, but this will depend on the circuit you are at. Some circuits will have firmer noise restrictions that others. Be aware that most circuits do not allow racing engines before 9am, so you may need to push your car around the paddock if you are called to scrutineering, for instance, and will not allow engine noise after say 6:30pm.

Once track action starts, pay close attention to your timetable and the paddock tannoy announcements. You will be called to the assembly area prior to your session, and although this will be marked on your paddock plan, it is worth familiarising yourself with the paddock layout as soon as you can, so you can navigate your way to the assembly area, parc ferme, scrutineering bay or pit lane, as requested. You can usually be called to the assembly area for your session anything up to 30 minutes before your session, to ensure all cars arrive in time. If the timetable allows, the day can sometimes run as much as 20 minutes ahead of schedule, so keep an eye on the time throughout the day and make sure you know which championship is on track before you, particularly if you cannot hear the tannoy announcements. Also allow time for noise testing prior to your first session.

Prior to heading to the assembly area, make sure you have all of your equipment, such as helmet, gloves, HANS or FHR device and wrist restraints (if applicable). You will already be wearing your race suit and boots before you get into your car, but some drivers may put the rest of their equipment on once in the assembly area. As you approach assembly, there will be a team of marshals to greet you, and they will tell you where you need to park. If you are heading out on-circuit for practice or qualifying, drivers will line up in the order they arrive in; however, if you are going out for a race, you will line up in your grid order, to make things a lot easier at the start of the race. In this case, markers with numbers on will be displayed around the assembly area, these numbers correspond to grid positions. As you arrive, marshals will cross you off their list and line you up in your correct starting position. They will also ask you if your pin is out – this refers to your fire extinguisher. Before getting in your car, make sure the pin on your fire extinguisher is out, in case it is needed in a hurry during the session or race.

Once everyone has lined up accordingly and the circuit is clear to proceed, you will be released onto the circuit. In the case of practice or qualifying your session will start as soon as you hit the circuit. Although you are immediately into a qualifying session, you can't expect to be at full speed right away. Common practise is to use the first lap on-circuit as an out lap, to allow your car, tyres and brakes to get up to temperature. Once you are comfortable and happy with your car, you can start to push to secure some quick laps. Qualifying sessions tend to be around 15 to 20 minutes long, which doesn't allow for coming into the pits to change setup for instance. If you do have friends or family with you, ask them to take a tyre pressure gauge to the pit lane with them. If time allows, mainly during a practice session, you may want to pit part way through to have your tyre pressures checked. Running on-circuit with the right tyre pressures for the conditions can be very beneficial. For a warm, dry track surface you will want to start with lower tyre pressures, as they will get hotter as you lap; however, for a wet track surface you will want to start with a higher tyre pressure. This is because the track surface is cold, so you artificially create a warm result by raising your tyre pressures.

Following qualifying, drivers will be directed into parc ferme by the officials. Once you are in parc ferme, strict conditions come info force. You cannot make any adjustments to your car, including checking tyre pressures. Although your friends, family or team can come and see you at parc ferme, they cannot enter or pass you any equipment for your car. The only time this would be permitted is if the scrutineering team who are in parc ferme with you ask to check part of your car that you will need mechanical equipment to get to. If you have a mechanical team supporting you, they will be able to enter parc ferme to do this for you, at the request of the scrutineer.

Before the start of the race, as mentioned above, you will once again head to the assembly area, although this time you will line up in your allocated grid position. As you head out onto the circuit, the course car, or safety car, will lead the way round to the grid, with all drivers staying in grid order, one behind the other. Once everyone has lined up in their grid slot, you will be shown a green flag and a 'formation lap' board, to signal the start of your formation lap. The formation lap gives drivers a chance to warm their tyres and get things up to temperature before the start of the race, so you are not starting on cold tyres. This is why when watching a race, you will see cars weaving back and forth on their formation lap, to ensure they get as much heat as possible into their tyres. It is also worth noting that although more often than not you will only do one formation lap, sometimes you may do two. This would only happen in the event your race conditions are different to that of your qualifying conditions. For example, if you qualifying session was dry, but race day was wet, you would be allocated two consecutive green flag, or formation, laps to adjust to the change in conditions. You will always be notified about this beforehand though, usually via a championship bulletin or your championship coordinator. Sometimes the lap from the assembly area to the grid will act as your green flag lap. Make sure to check your start procedure beforehand.

The race start will use lights, rather than a flag system. Whilst sitting on the grid you will be shown a one minute, followed by a 30 second board. This is to prepare you for the race start. Following this, the five red lights on the starting gantry will come on for a few seconds, once they turn off that is the signal to go. Although your eyes will be focused on the first corner at this point, try and be aware of stalled cars on the grid. If a car struggles to get away, marshals will wave a yellow flag from the pit wall (flag signals are discussed in more detail in the table below), as a warning to other drivers. In the event of a false start, cars will be re-gridded followed by another formation lap.

Once your race has finished, either by reaching its time if it is a timed race, or by completing the set number of laps, the chequered flag will signal the end of the session. Once you have passed the chequered flag, proceed around on a cool down lap before heading into the pit lane and parc ferme, like you did at the end of qualifying. Again, parc ferme conditions as described above will apply. Failing to comply with parc ferme conditions could result in you receiving a penalty.

What to be aware of – car racing

After discussing flag signals for track days and kart races, now we have the flag signals for car racing. There are some slight differences again. Karting uses some flags that are not commonly used in car racing; however, the majority of flags used in both remain the same. Again, some circuits will compliment their flag signals with light signals, to ensure drivers can see the message being communicated to them. Flag signals are there for the safety and wellbeing of all drivers and officials, so it is vitally important to pay attention to them. Those who do not pay attention to flag signals, even by pure accident, will find themselves in front of the Clerk of the Course. Depending on the severity of the offence, punishment will range from a slap on the wrist and a warning not to do it again, to a sizeable fine, points on your race licence, or exclusion from the result.

Flag signal	What it means	Where you will see it
Green flag	Signals that the circuit is clear and open. The green flag will also be used to indicate the start of the formation lap before the start of a race	At all marshal posts around the circuit
Stationary yellow flag	Slow down (to 60-70% of your normal speed) to ensure you have complete control of your vehicle, as there is an incident or hazard ahead. No overtaking	At marshal posts around the circuit
Waved yellow flag	Follow instructions as for stationary yellow flag above; however, a waved yellow flag indicates more danger as the hazard is directly ahead. Be prepared to deviate from your normal racing line to avoid any hazards	At the marshal posts nearest to the incident or hazard on the circuit
Red flag	No overtaking, slow your pace and return to the pit lane or start line. Do not suddenly stop on-circuit at the sight of a red flag. Watch out for officials as you approach the pit lane or starting grid, as they may be on-circuit to direct you	At all marshal posts around the circuit
Blue flag	The blue flag is to let you know there is a faster car coming through. It reminds drivers to look in their mirrors, as you could be impeding the car behind you. Pull to one side at the safest opportunity to allow the car to pass safely. In a race situation you are likely to be shown the blue flag if you are about to be lapped	At the relevant marshal posts around the circuit *(continues overleaf)*

Flag signal	What it means	Where you will see it
Black flag	The black flag indicates that you have done something wrong. You must return to the pit lane within one lap of seeing the black flag and report to the Clerk of the Course. A penalty may be enforced. You are usually given up to three chances to pass a black flag without reacting and coming into the pits before a stricter penalty is given, often exclusion	From the pit wall. The pit lane marshal will wave this at you from their position, usually together with a pit board displaying your race number
Black and white diagonal flag	Driving standards or track limits. You will be shown this flag if your standard of driving has fallen below acceptable. For example, if you are repeatedly driving beyond the edges of the track. You will be shown this a certain number of times before being given a time penalty. A time penalty will add time onto your race pace, which may drop you down the running order. If you continue to offend, you will be shown the black flag, so it is imperative you pay attention	From the pit wall. The pit lane marshal will wave this at you from their position on the pit wall, together with your race number
Red and yellow striped flag	This flag alerts you to something on the circuit, such as fluid or debris. It could be localised at one particular corner or in the case of fluid, it could be spread around the circuit. Proceed with caution	At the marshal post nearest to the fluid or debris, or at each post around the circuit if it has spread
Chequered flag	To signal the end of the session or race. Upon seeing the chequered flag, you will have one more lap, a cool down lap, after which you will be directed into the pit lane or into parc ferme. Do not continue to lap after the chequered flag has been shown, if you miss it and continue to lap the circuit, it shows you are not paying attention and you will receive a penalty	From the pit wall

Flag signal	What it means	Where you will see it
Union Jack	This is used to start a race in the absence of starting lights. It may also be used for mixed grid races. For example, when two different classes or championships are sharing a grid they may start at separate times, with the second grid setting off 20 seconds after the first. The grid at the front will start using the starting lights, whereas the grid at the rear will usually start upon the drop of the Union Jack	At the start line
Black flag with orange circle	To notify the driver there is an issue such as a mechanical failure or fire that they may not be aware of. This could also include loose bodywork. Return to the pits to have the issue rectified	From the pit wall
White flag	There is a slow moving vehicle on-circuit. This could be a slow moving car or a service vehicle, such as recovery or ambulance	At marshal posts around the circuit

I want to focus more on one of the points mentioned in the above table, track limits. This is something that has received a great deal of focus since around 2015, and it is now policed more than ever. Whether you are taking part in a track day, you are racing a kart or racing a car on-circuit, you must abide by the rules of track limits. Those who do not will be penalised. Track limits were enforced to ensure that no driver can gain an advantage by cutting the circuit or by using significant run off areas to gain on their fellow competitors. Track limits are defined by the usable area of the circuit, which is outlined by a painted white line and an (often) multicoloured kerb. The white line defines the edge of the circuit, with cars to be described as having left the circuit if any wheel crosses this white line. All circuits may differ on their position of track limits, as some may allow you to use the painted kerb beyond the white line without receiving a penalty. Any questionable area like this will usually be outlined in your driver's briefing or briefing notes. If you are unsure after seeing the circuit, you can always ask your club representatives or the Clerk of the Course to clarify the position on track limits for a specific corner.

For those who breach track limits rules, you will first be shown a black and white diagonal flag together with your race number from the pit wall. This first flag is a warning that you have been seen to be abusing track limits and you are now on the radar of the Clerk of the Course. However, once studied by the Clerk, they will determine whether you broke track limits rules in order to take avoidable action, this could be because of a fellow competitor having an incident in front of you, or debris on the circuit that you had to avoid, or whether it was carried out through lack of care and attention. In this case, the situation will be taken into consideration. However, should you be deemed to have flouted the track limits rules on purpose, you will then be shown the black and white flag again. You will usually be shown the warning flag a maximum of three times, after which you will be penalised. If you still abuse the track limits after your third flag, you will then be given a five second penalty, after that this will increase to a 10 second penalty, with these time penalties being added to your time at the end of the race. If you continue to offend, the next step is a drive through penalty – this means you will come into the pits, drive all the way through at the pit lane speed limit (usually 60km) before rejoining the circuit. After this you will be give a stop-go penalty; this means you will come into the pit lane, there is usually a penalty area marked out as you enter the pit lane for penalties such as this. You will have to stop for a specified amount of time, as timed by the officials, before being released to rejoin the race. If you continue to abuse the track limits after this, the final step is exclusion from the race. If you violate track limits during qualifying, the lap in which you offended will be deleted, and this could be your quickest lap.

One of the purposes of this book is to let you know what you can and cannot do, to hopefully make your transition into the motor racing world as simple and faultless as possible.

CHAPTER 5

SIMULATORS

When it comes to testing and preparing for races the first point of call is usually a track or test day. However, elements outside of our control can sometimes scupper this plan, whether it comes down to the weather stopping play, issues with your car, or the simple fact that you're unable to attend a circuit in person. In this instance, there is an alternative, for both kart and circuit drivers: using a professional driver performance centre. Although there is rarely a substitute for getting some seat time and practising on an actual circuit, the development in the technology behind simulators means that driver training in this way can still be highly beneficial.

Race simulators have always been a popular driving training tool, whether it is a home-based or professional setup. In recent years the technology behind race simulators has developed a great deal, and during the Covid-19 pandemic simulator training and racing advanced even further, and also increased in popularity. Given the restrictions in place, with social distancing and the fact that track and test days were unable to take place, racing drivers had to find other methods of training to ensure they maintained their competitive edge. Although professional simulator centres, such as those discussed within this chapter, were also forced to close during the restrictions, professionals within the simulator industry were able to use the technology available to them to enhance their services and training facilities. Everyone was forced to adapt to a new way of working, and race simulator providers seemed to thrive during the pandemic, and have been able to continue this momentum post-lockdown.

There is a vast selection and variety of simulators on the market, and which to choose will depend on your budget. Home simulators can be as basic or as high tech as you wish, depending on the space and facilities available. This can be something you put together yourself, or a more complex piece of equipment purchased ready to go from one of the main simulator distributors. In terms of professional simulators, there are three main simulator centres in the UK: Base Performance Simulators, iZone Driver Performance and SIMTrack Driver Performance Centre, which between them have the market pretty well covered. During this chapter I will discuss each of these centres in further detail, including the operational methods and benefits of each. Despite each of these centres ultimately offering the same goal, all three of them operate somewhat differently.

This chapter will also focus on home simulators, and the benefits and disadvantages of a home setup versus a professional centre. I want to clarify that simulators are not designed as a complete substitute for track time; however, the two elements work hand in hand. Skills that are learnt during a simulator session can be transferred to the circuit, and vice versa. This helps the driver to develop a vast array of skills.

Whether you just require some preparation ahead of your next race or you want to develop a career in motorsport, each of the three centres discussed below will have a programme that will suit you.

PROFESSIONAL DRIVER PERFORMANCE CENTRES IN THE UK
Base Performance Simulators

Base Performance Simulators (BPS) is one of two long standing driver performance centres in the UK. Owned and run under the watchful eye of professional racing driver, Darren Turner, Base Performance has a great deal of experience and expertise behind its design and operation process. Darren is one of the UK's most successful and experienced racing drivers. Having begun his career in single-seater racing, Darren fulfilled many years as test driver for the McLaren Formula One team, whilst also developing his racing career in touring cars and sports cars. Since 2005, Darren has been heavily involved with Aston Martin Racing. As well as contesting races with the Aston Martin Racing works team, and many of the marque's customer teams, Darren is also the high-performance development driver for Aston Martin Lagonda. With three 24 Hours of Le Mans race wins to his name, his knowledge and experience speaks for itself, and demonstrates the level of expertise behind the Base Performance brand.

Based in Banbury, the relatively central location of Base Performance makes it easily accessible by much of the UK. With 10 years of operation behind them, Base has established itself as one of the 'go-to' centres for driver development. As well as assisting drivers with their development and training in-house, Base also develops and builds professional simulators, for both professionals and amateurs, to be used in either a specialist or home setting.

As with countless businesses, during the Covid19 pandemic, Base was forced to adapt its operational strategy to reflect a change in the motorsport industry. The sudden growth in online and simulator racing, or iRacing, as well as remote driver training meant a business such as Base could utilise its home-based models to the best of its advantage.

The introduction of the home sim setup brings us nicely onto the Blade simulator rig. The Blade was designed and created by Base Performance, and it is something that was introduced in 2020. The ultimate home simulator system, the Blade is built on a specially-commissioned, rigid, powder-coated steel frame, this simulator boasts a BPS carbon, two-pedal, pedal box with electric fore/aft adjustment and a bespoke BPS carbon fibre race seat. Blade features the Precision Sim GPX Steering Wheel and runs a professional steering motor from Simucube; the Simucube 2 PRO provides 25nm of torque for the most realistic steering feel in simulation.

For sound and vision, Blade is supplied with a Cambridge Audio speaker system and Sennheiser headset plus a single 49in (125cm) curved Samsung monitor with 120hz refresh rate, creating a fully immersive driving experience. With a home simulation system such as the Blade, you can enjoy the professionalism that Base Performance has to offer, from the comfort of your own home. For those with a busy work-life schedule, a professional home simulator system such as this enables you to manage your driver training schedule, without needing time to squeeze in a track day, and with the wonders of technology, you can still do this and benefit from tuition, either from Base Performance or your own driver coach.

Facilities

For those looking to visit Base Performance, its in-house facility is very impressive, as you would expect. At the hands of a small, yet extremely experienced team of professionals, Base Performance tailors its simulator packages to meet the specific needs of the driver. Specialising in endurance racing for GT race cars and sports cars, BPS draws on the experience amassed by Darren Turner during his illustrious career so far.

Having a simulator model similar to what you will be racing is very advantageous. With that in mind, Base Performance has a single-seater simulator, and a GT simulator, to ensure it meets the needs of a wide variety of drivers, whether you decide to race in single-seater race cars or opt for the tin top route, you can develop your on-track performance with Base Performance. Even at club level, the benefits of a professional race simulator can be huge. For those who are racing a tin top or road style car, even something like a Caterham, the GT cockpit is an extremely useful tool. Although the cockpit you will be sat in is a GT chassis, the system is programmed to resemble a car and circuit that suits you, to ensure you get the most out of your session, and the feedback you receive from the brakes and steering system is second to none, and extremely realistic. The system is programmed with a wide variety of cars and circuits, to ensure you are fully prepared for your next race meeting. This is particularly appealing at club level, because as a novice driver each circuit you visit will more than likely be a completely new venue to you. Even if you have visited as a spectator, to drive the circuit is very different. At the moment, following the Covid19 pandemic, another fairly big change is the availability of track and test days. Given that circuits have been forced to close for so long during 2020 and the early stages of 2021, and the fact that drivers have missed out on so much track time, track days and test days have been selling out extremely quickly, usually within hours. Hopefully this will soon calm down as we start to resemble some sort of normality, but this is where a home simulator system comes into play. Not only do you save time and money booking a track day, together with saving on the tyres, fuel and other consumables you will use during a day on-circuit, you have the training system at your full disposal.

As well as appealing to racing drivers, Base Performance Simulators are heavily involved in corporate events. Whether the event is tailored to a business wanting to impress a new client, or perhaps offer its staff a team building experience, the professional facility that Base Performance has developed is the perfect setting. This is particularly useful for those drivers with sponsors, or perhaps those who are beginning to approach businesses. Having something such as a professional race simulator to offer may well enhance your portfolio and impress the business in question.

Simulator sessions

As I mentioned above, packages are tailored to the individual driver, to ensure each person benefits from their session in the simulator. Sessions with Base Performance are designed to ensure a driver has as much track time as possible, which can sometimes be limited during a track or test day, to enable the ability to hone their skills behind the wheel.

Simulator sessions held at Base Performance, are designed to allow the driver to learn the basics. Although there is a team of professionals on hand to assist the driver through his or her sessions, BPS have created the best environment they can to allow drivers to develop their skills, from learning the basics, such as racing lines to choosing a reference point on-circuit. Reference points are used by a driver to work out a braking point, for instance a corner marker or advertising board beside the circuit could be used to remind you where you need to brake and where to turn in for a corner. I have heard many stories over the years, particularly from the days of Sir Stirling Moss, where drivers have used spectators as braking points. This is all well and good until the spectator moves, unbeknown to the driver. Another particularly amusing story from a similar era is of a driver using a rock as a marker; however, the rock turned out to be a tortoise, which was edging slowly towards the corner, and therefore ruined his braking point. Each driver will use something that works for them, but make sure it is something that won't move.

The environment at BPS is such that a driver can bring their own driver coach with them, if they wish. Working with one particular driver coach certainly has its advantages, as each instructor will work slightly differently and use varying methods. Having your coach join you in the simulator means together you can replicate the work you have been doing at the circuit and continue that relationship in the virtual world. Being able to work with your driver coach during a track or test day as well as a simulator session helps to keep that continuity, and further enhances your development.

As mentioned earlier in this chapter, actual time on-circuit on a track or test day can be severely limited. Whether that is due to the number of stoppages due to other people's incidents, the weather causing issues or mechanical issues with your car, the total amount of time you spend on-circuit during a track or a sessioned test day can be extremely restricted. This is not the case with a simulator session, whether you book a one-hour slot, a half day or full day session, your time is only interrupted if you choose to have a break, for instance. If you want to spend your full session driving, you can, without the risk of unwanted delays. This applies to any simulator session.

Additional features
Not only does the racing experience that Darren Turner brings to Base Performance Simulators benefit the facility, but also the fact that he has 20 years of experience developing cutting-edge Formula One simulators. This understanding has been applied to every aspect of BPS, to ensure it releases the best, state-of-the-art technology available in the simulator industry.

As well as being applied to its in-house systems, BPS has used this knowledge to enhance its online coaching facilities. With face-to-face coaching put on hold during the Covid19 pandemic, online coaching became more advanced, with more and more drivers connecting with their driver coaches through an online medium. This, in turn, enhanced simulator sales for BPS, particularly with its Blade home simulator, as drivers and coaches would purchase a home simulator each, to work together and enhance their online training programme. During this time, the simulator building side of the BPS business expanded even further.

The simulators built by BPS are bespoke to the individual and tend to be purchased by amateur and professional drivers as well as race teams.

iZone Driver Performance
In similar fashion to Base, iZone Driver Performance has been in action for over 10 years. Founded by John Pratt and developed by experienced racing driver and triple World Touring Car Champion, Andy Priaulx, iZone Driver Performance has a powerful ethos, which captures the following values:

➤ Innovation
   Constant innovation ensures that drivers are never standing still in their training and development
➤ Individualised training
   iZone's training is focused on the opportunities identified in the driver's initial assessment
➤ Focused on skills
   Training is focused on the core skills that define a driver's method and their ability to perform
➤ Strength based
   iZone aims to transform your strengths and weaknesses into something more powerful
➤ Performing under pressure
   iZone developed drivers are trained to be mentally resilient, in order to execute the right skills at the right time, regardless of the pressure they face
➤ Being instinctive and naturally adaptive
   Drivers must adapt instinctively to new circuits, cars and changing levels of grip or handling

Based at Silverstone Circuit, within the business park located just outside the main gates of the circuit, iZone also enjoys a central location within the country, and with one of the most famous circuits in motorsport on its doorstep, it fully embraces the continuity between track time and simulator training. One of the most well-known professional simulator centres, and one of the first to introduce the simulator into motorsport training, iZone has a dedicated team of professionals working in various roles, to provide a thorough service to all calibres of driver. The iZone team consists of a Performance Director, Commercial Director and Performance Coach, Head of Sports Science, Performance Psychologist, Performance Coach and iZone Test Driver, Simulator Engineer and Personal Trainer and an Esports Manager, ensuring each area of expertise is managed.

A significant focus for iZone Driver Performance is to develop an 'all round' driver. As well as offering driver training on its state-of-the-art simulator, iZone focuses a great deal on the mind and body, to ensure drivers are not only physically prepared for their next race meeting, but also mentally prepared.

Although iZone is well-known for its simulator presence, one of the key elements the centre boasts is that the simulator gives the driver a controlled environment in which to learn during its training programmes, with the simulator acting as a tool within that training programme.

Part of the method behind the iZone driver training courses teach drivers that their practice must be purposeful, instilling true intrinsic values in each driver. As part of a driver's personal performance and preparation, iZone teaches the

80/20 rule, which effectively translates to the fact that 80% of what you will do at a circuit can be carried away from the venue in your simulator training session, whilst the other 20% you have no control over. Elements such as the weather, the car or other drivers all contribute to this 20%, as you can't control the things that may put a stop to your day on-circuit. The iZone team also works with drivers on understanding the methodology behind being quick on-circuit.

One of the courses that iZone Driver Performance offers is a structured monthly programme. As a new customer to iZone, drivers are invited to take part in a series of introductory sessions, as part of an initial trial period. These sessions take place over the course of a week and introduce you to every aspect that iZone has to offer, together with the type of training you will likely receive. If you wish to continue with this programme after your trial week you can develop this further, for a cost of £25 per week. Alternatively, you can book individual sessions to use some of the centre's facilities on an ad hoc basis.

The structured monthly development programme, as mentioned above, is designed to provide drivers with a defined training agenda, which can be monitored and discussed on an ongoing weekly basis. Again, another business that has managed to utilise online facilities during restrictions enforced by Covid19, drivers can either take part in this programme remotely or in-house at their Silverstone base.

Separated into two sections, this course offers simulator skill training and access to the iZone Performance Clinic. Focusing on the first point, the simulator skill training segment concentrates on driving skill. The structure of the training within this section is based on the strengths and weaknesses identified during your initial assessment. This assessment is nothing to worry about, it is purely to allow the iZone team to find out more about you as a driver and discover what it is you want to gain from your training with them. The assessment will involve:

➤ Understanding your background and motorsport CV so far (this is just as much for beginners as those who want to develop the skills they already have, so don't worry if you don't yet have a motorsport CV)
➤ Understanding your goals – short, medium and long-term
➤ A detailed assessment of your strengths and weaknesses
➤ Technical and tactical skills, your mental resilience and fitness and psychomotor skills

The information gathered during this assessment will enable the iZone team to create your training goals for the month ahead.

As part of the simulator training skill portion of the course, the teaching method focuses on skills that promote a natural driving ability. By focusing on natural ability, this ensures that drivers are skilled, conditioned under pressure and very adaptable to different situations when on-circuit. It also ensures drivers are comfortable within unpredictable situations and able to perform on demand. A situation where this might apply, is the ability to record a strong qualifying lap at a moment's notice. For example, if you have three laps for qualifying, this will consist of an out lap, a flying lap, which will be your qualifying lap, and an in lap back to the pits. Being able to perform in these conditions is somewhat stressful and demanding; however, with this conditioned training it enables you as a driver to focus during this situation and perform immediately. Simulator skill training focuses on the following areas:

➤ Eye tracking and vision training
➤ General technique, such as braking, racing lines, throttle use
➤ Creating automaticity (the ability to carry out a task automatically without thinking, usually as a result of practice and repetition, as taught at iZone)
➤ Wet driving
➤ Qualifying
➤ Race starts, first few laps, defending and overtaking
➤ Stress exposure training
➤ Race and test planning and reviewing

All of these are transferable between the simulator and the race circuit, meaning you can take the skills learned in the simulator and apply them to your next test day, qualifying session or race.

The second part discusses what's available in iZone's unique Performance Clinic. The Performance Clinic is a daily remote training programme covering a wide range of skills from racing technique and fitness training to mental skills, mindfulness practice, visualisation, iRacing and performance profiling. A typical schedule looks like this:

• **Daily Performance and Mindfulness Clinic**
  Monday to Friday – 08:30 for 90 minutes
• **Remote Fitness Training**
  Monday, Wednesday and Thursday – 16:30 for 60 minutes
• **Mindfulness Training**
  Monday – 18:00 for 60 minutes
• **iRacing**
  Wednesday – 19:30 for 60 minutes
• **Open Forum Q & A Session**
  Thursday – 09:00 for 30 minutes
• **Performance Profiling**
  End of every month

For those who cannot commit to the morning sessions, due to work commitments for instance, these sessions are recorded for you watch back later, so you don't have to miss out.

Facilities and sim sessions

Included within the impressive iZone Driver Performance centre are five high tech simulators, three of which are car simulators and two simulators dedicated to karting. The facility also hosts a motorsport gym, an esports zone, and a mind and yoga room.

With regard to simulators, iZone can offer training for drivers of all ages, levels and ability. The three simulators aimed at car racing consist of two single-seater and one GT simulator, enabling the centre to offer training for drivers in everything from club level racing through to international sports cars. All car models used on the three car simulators are developed in-house at iZone with circuits laser scanned and constantly kept up to date. Each simulator includes live data, comprehensive recording and analysis software, eye tracking, heart rate monitoring and biometric/EEG feedback to assist with more advanced training methods.

In order to create a simulator facility for karters, iZone and KartSim joined forces to provide karters with the opportunity to benefit from simulator training, using the latest kart simulator technology in start-of-the-art surroundings. As well as simulator training sessions, the kart simulator programmes are tailored to young karters, offering after school programmes to fit in with their schedule.

A particularly unique feature of the iZone kart simulator is the kart to car transition programme. If you are progressing from kart racing to car racing, the iZone transition coaching course will help with that somewhat difficult period as you adjust to new surroundings. This is also a good way to prepare yourself, before jumping straight into a car on a live circuit, particularly if you are slightly anxious about the process. Whether you are moving into single-seater cars or tin tops, the kart to car transition programme will assist in adapting what you have learnt in karting, teach you new skills that you can apply to car racing, as well as guide you around some new circuits.

If you are at the very start of your karting or car racing journey, iZone have introduced a range of courses, designed to help with that initial process. The ARKS training programme assists those looking to acquire their karting licence, whilst the ARDS training provides support to those aiming to become a car racing driver. Both programmes have been designed together with Motorsport UK, to help guide drivers through the initial steps, from before taking their respective licence test, through to their first test and race meetings. This programme will help prepare you for the practical element of your ARKS or ARDS licence test.

As well as remote training for both karters and car racing drivers, iZone offers a two-day course aimed at International drivers, assisting drivers of all experience levels all over the world. With each of the training programmes that iZone offers, there is also a physical training element and a focus on performance psychology, to ensure all drivers are physically and mentally prepared for the task ahead.

Drivers who visit the iZone facility in person will have the opportunity to use the high-tech gym equipment. You can book a one-to-one training session with one of the centre's trainers to transform your fitness levels to that of a fully-fledged motorsport athlete. An initial assessment will indicate which areas of fitness you would like to focus on, so a bespoke training regime can be created for you. As well as physical fitness, this will also work on your nutrition and sleep activity. During your fitness training session, you will cover the following:

> Personal training for the gym and on-circuit
> Psychomotor block sessions
> Strength block sessions
> Psychomotor sessions
> Strength sessions
> Brake training
> Pre-performance routine
> Nutrition
> Bespoke gym training programme

As well as the information discussed above, iZone is also able to offer remote simulator training, with a bespoke programme that provides one-to-one driver coaching through an online service.

Main benefits of iZone Driver Performance

The vast array of facilities that iZone Driver Performance has available is certainly beneficial. With so many training opportunities in one place, it means you can spend a day at iZone and not only develop your race performance, but also enhance your mind and body fitness.

SIMTrack Driver Performance Centre

SIMTrack is the newest of the UK's main professional driver performance centres, having celebrated its second birthday in January 2021. Despite still being in its infancy, SIMTrack has already cemented itself as a key contender when it comes to a professional and competitive facility. Owned and run by racing driver and businessman, Adam Croft, SIMTrack provides an unrivalled simulator experience for drivers of all experience levels and abilities. Based at Ginetta Cars

SIMTrack's racing simulator suite, with race car chassis and six metre panoramic screen. (Courtesy SIMTrack)

headquarters in Garforth, Leeds, SIMTrack is the only centre of its type in the North of England. Being situated much further north than its competitors gives SIMTrack easy access to a whole host of racing drivers and teams who are based North of the Midlands, whilst successfully bridging a gap between motorsport drivers of all experience levels.

Despite only being in its third year of existence, SIMTrack has already built a strong customer base, with customers ranging from those competing in the 750 Motor Club Type R Trophy and Bikesports Championship, to experienced racing drivers contesting the likes of the World Endurance Championship and competing at the highest level of the sport.

The personnel behind SIMTrack have developed and expanded much of the operating system behind its state-of-the-art facility themselves, to ensure the simulator caters for as many championships and drivers as possible. Focusing on the worldwide notion of motorsport, you can sample every circuit from Croft Circuit (North Yorkshire) to Mount Fuji (Japan). The content is extremely vast and accurate.

During the first year of business, the brains behind SIMTrack Driver Performance Centre, championship winning racing driver, Adam Croft, decided to develop the technology further, to appeal to the wider audience. Using his own Caterham race car as the model, he was able to programme content from his race car into the simulator to a realistic level. Data gathered from the race track transferred into the simulator computer, to give accurate feedback for the driver.

Armed with interchangeable chassis, SIMTrack offers a varied experience for drivers of all levels and abilities, from junior drivers and club level motorsport through to World Endurance Championship racers who are racing at the highest level possible.

Facilities

In order to appeal to the needs of each customer who walks through the door, whether you are a novice driver about to embark on your first experience of racing, or a seasoned professional, SIMTrack has superb facilities to suit your developmental needs. With a choice of two interchangeable chassis, depending on what you want to achieve from your session, each system is a purpose-built racing car chassis to reflect a huge range of different race cars, from entry level club racing sports cars, through to top end GT machinery and prototypes.

In terms of the chassis available with SIMTrack you can select either an Aston Martin GT3 chassis or a Ginetta G40 cockpit. Both chassis are equipped with market-leading simulator hardware, including force feedback steering, full brake and clutch assemblies, a quick release steering wheel, dashboard display and racing pedal box. Together, regardless of the cockpit you select, the feedback from the machinery emulates a normal race car perfectly, making this the ideal driver training component.

Aside from the two professional simulator chassis, the SIMTrack facility comprises a bespoke racing simulator suite with a six metre panoramic screen and a data engineering room, and top end technology that provides simulations of over 100 circuits from across the world, as well as an extensive library of race cars, from single-seaters to GT race cars. Although it seems as though there is a heavy focus on GT and tin top racing development at SIMTrack, if you are racing a single-seater, do not be deterred. Although the cockpits used are of a tin top design, the high-end simulator software used within the facility is still heavily suited and appealing to single-seater drivers.

As well as its impressive in-house training facility, SIMTrack is now also an official re-seller for the Base Performance Simulators Blade bespoke customer racing simulator, as discussed under the 'Base Performance Simulators' section. Used by a number of professional racing drivers and top-flight simulator racers, the Blade is the ultimate in home simulation. More high-end than many home simulator systems on the market, the Blade sits at the higher end of the budget scale; however, it is a superb piece of machinery and worthy of the price tag.

Although simulators are a useful training tool for drivers amongst the ranks of club racing, they have proven particularly useful for those drivers who are racing on an international scale. With the likes of SIMTrack, professional, experienced and well-known drivers, such as Guy Smith and Mike Simpson regularly use the SIMTrack Driver Performance facility as part of their main training regime. Both Guy and Mike compete on an international level, but experience of circuits in Europe, America and Asia is difficult to come by. It's not like just popping to Donington Park for a mid-week track day, there are a lot of implications when it comes to arranging international test days. Use of a simulator beforehand is the ideal preparation, providing invaluable experience.

A very realistic experience in the car at SIMTrack. (Courtesy SIMTrack)

Sim sessions

SIMTrack offers a variety of simulator session options, from full season packages to bespoke bundles and also corporate events. More often than not a driver will attend for a one-to-one session; however, sometimes one or two drivers may attend together to share a session with one driver coach. SIMTrack has the added benefit of its in-house driver coach, multiple Ginetta champion and current GT cup racer, James Kellett, on hand for all sessions.

Although some sessions may just be an hour-long, each session is tailored to the individual, to ensure your specific needs are met. Each driver will want to achieve something in particular from a session in the simulator, and SIMTrack is more than happy to accommodate this. You can even brush up on your wet weather driving skills in the simulator, meaning you really can prepare for all eventualities.

As mentioned above, SIMTrack can also create a full season package, which includes training before each round of your respective championship or series. Having regular training in this way will certainly impact on your development as a driver, whether you opt for pure simulator training or a combined schedule of simulator and on-track practice, the two will complement one another perfectly.

Data loggers, such as those discussed in Chapter 4 can also be used in your simulator session, so you won't miss out on your data. However, the system does also create telemetry for the data engineer to analyse and discuss at length with you, similar to that of a test session.

To book a standard session, you can do this on the SIMTrack Driver Performance Facebook page; however, if you would prefer a more bespoke package, you can email or call SIMTrack directly, to arrange something more suited to your training needs.

Main benefits of SIMTrack

The SIMTrack Driver Performance facility certainly benefits its drivers. It is extremely professional, and the small team behind the SIMTrack name means the service you receive is second to none. Its location is certainly a positive note, not only being based at Ginetta Cars headquarters, but the fact that it is the only centre of its type in the North of England opens it up to a whole host of racing drivers, who maybe are unable to drive further south to the likes of iZone Driver Performance and Base Performance Simulators.

Although being based at Ginetta Cars means SIMTrack has access to a vast amount of racing drivers, the facility also works very independently, opening itself up to drivers from all championship and series, both in the UK and internationally.

KartSim

There are plenty of single-seater, tin top and GT car racing simulators available within the industry, but what about karting? The most popular company offering simulation training for those in the karting world is KartSim. KartSim provides high-quality, professional simulators and simulation software to kart racers looking to improve and perfect their on-track ability.

In terms of the software developed by KartSim, it features kart models and circuits popular amongst the UK and European kart racing market, in a bid to help drivers develop their skills. Initially released in 2017, the products and software available through KartSim have developed a great deal, in order to maintain a competitive edge within the karting industry.

Using Lidar data, the circuits that appear on the KartSim software provide a high level of accuracy compared to the real thing. With information collected from aerial shots, the software allows the tarmac, elevation changes and track surface elements to be recorded and ensure an element of realism for the karter. The kart models included on the programme are created using real life data from various areas of a kart, such as engine and tyres. This gives the karter as real an experience as possible, without going to an actual kart track.

As well as professional software, KartSim develops a range of simulators to suit all budgets and experience levels. As mentioned under the iZone Driver Performance information, KartSim works closely with iZone to provide the kart simulators and software in its two kart specific simulators. Together with providing professional centres with simulator equipment, KartSim also sells smaller simulator rigs, suitable for home use.

Designed specifically for the karting industry, KartSim rigs have been created to offer a life-like experience for karters away from the circuit. With a turn-key operation, mirroring your kart, you will experience full familiarity from the minute you climb aboard. Much like climbing into a GT or single-seater cockpit at the likes of Base Performance, iZone or SIMTrack to carry out some car racing training, the KartSim is built to emulate an actual kart. With braking feedback and overall dynamics matching that of your circuit kart, you will easily be able to prepare for your next big race away from the circuit.

The KartSim Pro Simulator is available in two different models, the Cadet or Junior model, or as a Senior kart chassis. Included with the simulator chassis is the following:

> ➤ Adjustable seat, steering column and feet
> ➤ Integrated high quality direct drive force feedback steering motor
> ➤ Integrated KartSim braking and power sensor package with adjustable kart pedals
> ➤ One year manufacturer's warranty and technical support
> ➤ Optional extras include:
>> ➢ Choice of KartSim software packages
>> ➢ Choice of KartSim gaming PC with KartSim telemetry software
>> ➢ Choice of single or triple screen options with custom built stands
>> ➢ Ability to upgrade to KartSim ultimate motion Platform
>> ➢ Ability to upgrade to KartSim ultimate seat vibration system
>> ➢ Ability to upgrade to KartSim ultimate seat virtual reality system

The price is configured on the KartSim website, depending on the options you would like included.

KartSim also produces a home simulator rig, aimed to assist those who are progressing from kart racing to single-seater racing; however, it is also suitable for those currently racing in a single-seater championship or series. The KartSim Formula Simulator has been designed and built to mirror your car in every way possible, from driving position to the feedback from the pedals and steering.

From its Silverstone base, KartSim offers professional coaching on site, as well as remote tuition for those drivers looking to develop their driving ability that bit further. KartSim is a superb training tool for those in the karting industry.

Bove Fabrications

There are many names in the world of home simulator rigs and systems, but one I'd particularly like to mention is Bove Fabrications. Although fairly new to the simulator industry, the names behind the Bove name have been involved in the motor racing industry for many years, mainly amongst the track day fraternity.

Based on the Caterham car, Bove Fabrications has created its own simulator rig, entitled the SIM Seven. The rig emulates the Caterham perfectly, from the outer finish to the realistic race car cockpit design and functionality, giving you a sense of realism.

The SIM Seven is designed for professionals or amateurs and is suitable for home use or corporate events. You can even create a bespoke design, selecting the colour of each element yourself, or mirror the look of your own race car or your favourite race car livery in the overall finish.

In terms of functionality, your gaming PC is located, and easily accessed, in the rear of the cockpit, behind the seat. All wiring is completely hidden, making it very home-user friendly, as there are no trailing cables to act as a potential hazard. The wheel mount is rigid and adjustable for height and rake. The pedal in the SIM Seven also allows for ample fore and aft movements, and well as height adjustability. Although there are a number of seat choices with the SIM Seven, the starter seat is the GRP unit, which is both sturdy and comfortable. Available in two different specifications, the SIM Seven Clubman and the SIM Seven Pro, this rig is again designed to suit varying skill levels, whilst remaining budget friendly.

HOW TO BENEFIT FROM A PROFESSIONAL SIMULATOR CENTRE

As you can see from the information detailed earlier in this chapter, although professional simulator centres each offer the same basic principle, there is a great deal more to professional simulator training than many drivers will realise.

In the same way as when you book a track or test day, you want to get the most out of your experience, and fully benefit from the day or session. This also applies to booking a session at a professional driver performance centre.

There are many benefits to booking a simulator session over a track or test day, and there are benefits to booking a track or test day over a simulator session; however, the two experiences go hand in hand. Considering a race simulator, when you make a booking, sessions tend to be available in one-hour or two-hour slots, half-day or full-day sessions. The benefit of this over a track day is that one or two hours or even a half day session can fit into your schedule much more easily than a full day on-circuit, and your training time won't be interrupted by weather conditions, stoppages or other external factors out of your control, meaning you can learn a great deal in your one hour simulator slot.

Visiting a professional centre for a simulator session certainly has a favourable outcome. There is a lot to be said for having a team of trained professionals from the motorsport industry at your disposal, whether that is a qualified instructor to guide you around the circuit lap after lap, or a trained data engineer to go through the more detailed technical information from your session. Having this level of professionalism at your fingertips is greatly beneficial and rewarding; you will witness this as you transfer the information learned in your simulator session onto the circuit. The extra assistance from a driver coach and data engineer is also included in the cost of the session, rather than this being an additional expense on top of your session, as with a track or test day.

A professional driver performance centre versus home sim setup

Professional simulator centres do hold an advantage over a home system, but don't immediately dismiss a home simulator system, as there are some perks to be enjoyed.

The initial obvious advantage of having a simulator set up at home is it is there at your disposal, to use as and when you like. Although there is the initial cost of the system, you don't then have to pay each time you use it, or pay for equipment such as fuel, tyres and brake pads, for instance. However, the chance to have a team of professionals to rally around you during a professional level session does certainly have its benefits. As previously mentioned, you will usually have an instructor on hand throughout your session, whether it is your regular coach or a professional provided by the simulator centre, you will also usually have a data engineer at your disposal, and technical support to look after the system, at the absolute minimum. The advances in online coaching may now mean you can experience remote coaching from your home simulator via an online system, although technical support may be in short supply.

Simulators and driver coaching

As discussed throughout the professional driver performance centre section of this chapter, if you have a particular driver coach who you work with on-circuit, you are usually more than welcome to take your coach with you to a simulator session, to ensure you can continue your training schedule. As you reach a more confident level, this can be a good opportunity to practise some more in depth skills, which you can then apply to your next track session. Simulator sessions are a good opportunity to practise a whole host of techniques, without the added threat of running off circuit. For those who are still building your confidence, the simulator is the ideal training ground for this.

Although the likes of Base Performance Simulators and iZone Driver Performance have been in existence for at least 10 years, using a simulator as a driver training tool can be a new concept for some driver coaches. As with most of today's new technology, you will find that many of the younger racing drivers progressing through the ranks will be effectively brought up on this sort of technology as a successful driver training tool, with others adapting to this new way of working.

Some instructors (very few) will not see the advantages of using such a system as an effective driver training tool in their day-to-day coaching; however, don't be disheartened if your driver coach tries to deter you from using a simulator. Although there is little substitute for learning to race by physically driving a car on-circuit, the simulator will teach you the basic skills needed to perfect your racing lines, braking points and pedal control, so it is highly recommended trying it at least once. Obviously if you plan to use a simulator, whether a professional driver performance centre or a smaller, home-based system, this will of course increase your budget, which is something to consider. The three centres discussed in this chapter will be able to create a bespoke package for you, depending on what you would like to gain from your session, so it is always worth speaking to them directly, rather than dismissing the idea completely due to budget restraints.

SIM RACING

Sim racing has increased tenfold in the last year. Again, since the Covid19 pandemic, this is another field that has been affected; however, instead of suffering a negative effect, sim racing has blossomed.

As the country went into lockdown, Motorsport UK was forced to revoke any permits for motor racing events. For drivers, not only in the UK, but all over the world, this presented a problem. Whether it affected the club racer who was unable to get out and practise on a track day, a professional racing driver, or a driver coach who suffered from a distinct lack of income due to drivers no longer needing tuition, the motorsport front was suddenly somewhat dismal for many.

With that came the development of sim racing. This has been a popular online activity for many people, whether they aspire to become a racing driver, or they are a gamer who enjoys a bit of online car racing, although it definitely boomed during 2020. With so many high-profile racing drivers out of action, they found solace in the realms of sim racing.

There were many national and international competitions that were created, one in particular being from the British GT Championship, who created an Esports Championship. Welcoming drivers from across the world of motorsport, the British GT Esports Championship took place over a number of weekends at circuits across the UK. With a championship battle open for drivers in either GT3 or GT4, as in the regular British GT Championship, entry numbers came in abundance. The various Esports championships also created work for motorsport photographers, who were able to develop some of the online imagery. Something of this nature will likely become a regular off-season activity.

In recent years, sim racing has proven extremely beneficial for one driver in particular. Although there has always been a spot of cynicism around sim racers transferring to real world motorsport, one driver made this a success. Successful sim racer, James Baldwin was given the opportunity to race in the British GT Championship in 2020, and after winning the opening round, he proved that it can be done. Although being offered an opportunity such as this is not a regular occurrence, it worked out well for James.

Sim racing is certainly one of those elements that has developed in recent years, and with the improvement in technology, it will likely continue to grow after the latest surge.

CHAPTER 6

THE MEDIA

As the title suggests, in this chapter we will focus on media within motorsport. There are a number of different areas of the media to consider and be aware of. Over the years this has changed dramatically, with print media gradually being trumped by the likes of online media, such as web-based news, live streaming facilities, and social media. Even at club level, the media holds an important role in motorsport. Throughout this chapter I will discuss the various media outlets available to you, what to be aware of and how to use them to your advantage.

SOCIAL MEDIA

Let's start with one of the most prominent areas of modern media. Social media is an immensely powerful tool. It has certainly become a part of everyday life in more recent years, and it is an instrument that is constantly evolving. However, it is something that needs to be used correctly, particularly if you are aiming to climb the motorsport ladder, and once you are in the limelight. Whether you are just beginning your motorsport journey, or you are more accomplished in the sport, you need to be aware of the implications of your actions on social media. One of the best rules to follow – very simply, if you're unsure, don't hit post, and certainly do not post when angry. Let the post-race red mist settle before taking to Facebook.

Some of the information within this section will be more relevant to those further down the motorsport path, for instance those who are looking for sponsorship to help fund their racing, or those who have been racing a few years and are now progressing to the next level. But the basics of correct social media use are worth bearing in mind, even at the start of your journey.

Social media is constantly developing, and with so many different platforms available it's often difficult to decide which is the best method of communication for you. It largely depends on who you want to reach and the image you would like to portray. Facebook, Instagram and Twitter are the most professional social media platforms, whereas SnapChat and TikTok will reach a different audience. Both may be great for personal use, but perhaps not for professional use, depending on the activity you are sharing. There is of course LinkedIn as well, a superb platform for drivers and teams that portrays a very professional image; it is also a fantastic way of connecting with potential sponsors. Whichever platform you decide to use, always remember who can see your information and posts. If you want to be seen, of course, you will want to ensure posts are set to public rather than private, but remember that allows potential sponsors, team bosses and fellow drivers to follow your story as well. Be sensible with your posts, and always keep them relevant.

When joining a racing club, make yourself familiar with the club's social media policy. Every organisation will have one, to ensure its members are not detrimental to either fellow competitors or the club on a public platform. The repercussions of a negative post can have extremely damaging effects to multiple people, yourself included. To reiterate my earlier point, if you are unsure, don't hit post.

As discussed in an earlier chapter, social media can be helpful when interacting with your fellow competitors, whether you are planning to attend a track or test day together, discussing your most recent race or looking for a bit of technical advice, it's a great way to connect with like-minded people. Social media platforms appear to have replaced forums in this respect, and with groups and pages for just about everything, you can usually find just what you're looking for in a matter of minutes.

Professional social media

As you progress through the ranks of motorsport you will likely reach a point where you want to create a more professional appearance on social media, especially if you are seeking sponsorship. You may even just want to create a space where you can share your racing exploits, without bombarding your personal account and those contacts who perhaps don't fall under the category of 'racing fans'.

More often than not, the first port of call is to create a Facebook business page, and it does have many advantages. It's free, as opposed to building a website, you can make it as professional or informal as you wish, and you can update it easily right from the paddock (providing you have a smartphone).

Facebook is usually the main port of call for setting up a business page, although you can now also choose to create a business account on Instagram. The look of a normal and business account on Instagram is largely the same, but there are some advantages to selecting business over personal. For one, it means you can choose to keep your personal account as private as possible, and limit who sees your content, but also, as with Facebook, it gives a more professional image. Potential sponsors want to look at your social media and see that you are a professional and marketable prospect, and they want to see relevant photos. Keep the 'night out' photos to your private, personal account.

Another benefit is that a business account, regardless of the platform you use, will enable you to view insights and data relating to your page. This is great for seeing which posts work, and which don't, and also the amount and type of people you are appealing to. It also enables you to utilise boosted posts or paid page promotions. You can either promote your page as a whole to the relevant audience, or you can boost individual posts for a small fee, selecting the precise audience you want to see your news. Boosted posts can be used on both Facebook and Instagram. You can also link the two pages together, so when you post on one it automatically posts on the other, a useful time saver. However, just be aware that not all posts transfer from one to the other smoothly. If you have tagged a sponsor or potential partner, their handle may differ slightly between the two platforms. Another useful social media tool is the 'stories' feature. This is great, especially for those smaller moments. Perhaps you are loading up ready to head off to a race meeting, share this on your story, both on Facebook and Instagram. It keeps your name and profile in the public eye.

One more thing, with regard to photographs, if your championship has its own professional photographer, I would highly recommend purchasing photos after each round. I can't tell you how important professional looking photos are on social media. It increases your level of professionalism tenfold.

Again, I want to reiterate the point to always bear in mind your championship or club's social media policy when posting your race weekend updates, regardless of whether you are using your personal account or a business platform.

Probably the most professional social media outlet available, in my opinion, is LinkedIn. As mentioned above, LinkedIn is heavily business orientated. As with all other social media platforms, LinkedIn has developed over the years, although it is still heavily corporate and business related, it also allows you to post individual updates, similar to that of Facebook or Twitter, rather than it just being a static page that displays your work experience. This enables you to show constantly updated information to those people or businesses you are hoping to connect with, which in turn demonstrates how current your activity is. It is important to keep your posts as up-to-date as possible, whether you are using Facebook, LinkedIn, Instagram or Twitter. There is nothing worse than looking at someone's business or racing driver page on social media and seeing it hasn't been updated for months.

For those looking to reach out to sponsors, LinkedIn is a superb networking platform, that will allow you to connect with potential sponsors. As with all other public material, just make sure it stays professional. Always remember in this instance to separate your personal and professional updates and information.

PRINT AND ONLINE MEDIA

You will often hear that print media is a dying art form, which I find very sad, but it is still very much a part of motorsport. With the likes of *Autosport* magazine (now in its 70th year), *Motorsport News* and *Motorsport* magazine, to name just three of the more prominent motorsport publications, still going strong, covering both national and international realms of the sport, there is always something to read. For those on the track side of the fence, it's still very much an honour to be included amongst the glossy pages of *Autosport*, and also extremely exciting. I have witnessed many excited drivers over the years dashing to their local supermarket on the Thursday after a race meeting to see if they made the cut. It never gets boring seeing your name in print, and I guarantee you will be just as excited the first time you read a race report in *Autosport* magazine bearing your name.

These main print publications will usually have a reporter in attendance at each race meeting, whether this is a freelancer or a member of its editorial staff, you'll seldom see a race meeting that's not covered. As you can imagine, space in a magazine can sometimes be something of a luxury in the middle of the race season, especially when you have the likes of BTCC, British GT and all manner of racing clubs in action all on the same weekend, so some coverage may be more limited than others, don't expect a full page spread every weekend. Some news reports will appear on the *Autosport* website, so don't be too disheartened if you didn't make the print cut, you may still be an online news sensation.

Those drivers that finish towards the sharp end of the race results, usually the top three, are likely to be collared for a few words of wisdom after the race. A word of advice – always make time to speak to the motorsport journalists. Speaking as a former motorsport journalist, the drivers that are more approachable and talkative are the drivers that will get approached more often for quotes and news, and in return you'll see your name in print. This in turn will help when the time comes to chase potential sponsors. If you have a good, strong media presence, it is more appealing to those businesses you are approaching. Companies want someone who is marketable, and who they can put out in front of their guests in any situation to promote their brand. You will see media training courses available within motorsport, which will teach you how to speak to the media and present yourself in front of the cameras, which in this business, is a useful tool to have. SIMTrack Driver Performance Centre hosts a media training course for drivers taking part in the Ginetta Junior Championship each year, whilst iZone Driver Performance also offers media training for drivers looking to enhance their public presence.

It is also worth getting to know your local press. Smaller publications, such as your local magazines and newspapers love a local story, and something like

Motorsport publications: still some of the best sources for motorsport news and the latest race reports – you may even see your name in print. (Courtesy Motorsport Images)

motorsport stands out against the more 'regular' sports stories, as it always appears different and exciting. Again, this will help when contacting local businesses about potential sponsorship. Demonstrating you have a strong media presence can be a strong selling point.

LIVE STREAMING

Live streaming has become a regular feature of motorsport in recent years, particular in 2020 when most motor racing events were forced to run behind closed doors. It meant racing fans, drivers' families and sponsors could still enjoy the action from the comfort of their living room.

The likes of the British Touring Car Championship and the British GT Championship have shown live coverage of their races for a number of years, either on their respective YouTube channels or television. However, during the last couple of years this has filtered down to club level motorsport.

Clubs such as the 750 Motor Club started live streaming a number of their race meetings through the Alpha Live streaming service. You will have read about Alpha Timing in Chapter Two, as it supplies club management and timing systems for karting; however, it also runs a successful live streaming service, serving both karting and car racing, through their broadcasting company.

In the case of the 750MC race events, Alpha Live not only provides a high quality live streaming service of all races, but they will also edit the footage into individual championships and series, for you to share on your social media platforms, with friends and family, or to send to sponsors. Being able to offer live coverage of your races is a great addition to your sponsorship proposal.

Other clubs have since followed suit, with now many of the main motorsport clubs offering a live streaming service. This may not be available for all clubs, championships and series, as it tends to be reserved for the more premium action. It is rather expensive, so it may also be that some clubs only supply live coverage of a number of their races throughout the season. For example, in the case of the Caterham Graduates Racing Club, a selection of their races will be streamed live on the BARC YouTube channel throughout the season. The likes of the BARC and the BRSCC also include highlights programmes, either on their respective YouTube channels, or on television via the free Front Runner channel.

Now, at the end of *So, You Want to be a Racing Driver?*, I hope you have found this book useful. Armed with everything you need to know to become a racing driver, whether on a more professional scale, with dreams of reaching the dizzying heights of Formula One or the 24 Hours of Le Mans, or more as a hobby, you are fully equipped to take on the world of motorsport. I look forward to seeing you on the grid very soon. Happy racing!

KART TEST AND RACE DAY CHECK LIST

Use this check list each time you are heading to a circuit, whether it is for a track day, test day or a race meeting, and you will never forget your equipment:

- ➤ Pre-event Admin:
    - ➢ Pay for race entry
    - ➢ Sign on online
    - ➢ Email a photo of race licence to organising club
    - ➢ Scrutineering declaration

- ➤ Admin:
    - ➢ Tickets (print e-tickets for MSV circuits beforehand)
    - ➢ Paddock pass (if applicable)
    - ➢ MSUK race licence (make sure it is signed)
    - ➢ Upgrade card
    - ➢ Blue Book
    - ➢ A copy of the final instructions (distributed by your organising club)
    - ➢ A printed timetable for the event (applicable to test days and race meetings)

- ➤ Racing Equipment:
    - ➢ Race suit
    - ➢ Helmet
    - ➢ Balaclava
    - ➢ Gloves
    - ➢ Boots
    - ➢ Fireproof underwear
    - ➢ Neck collar (if applicable)

➤ Mechanical Equipment
  ➢ Tools
  ➢ Axle stands
  ➢ Jack
  ➢ Cable ties
  ➢ Gaffer tape
  ➢ Blue roll
  ➢ Tyre pressure gauge
  ➢ Fuel and jerry cans

➤ Other Equipment
  ➢ Pop up awning
  ➢ Ratchet straps
  ➢ Electrical cables
  ➢ Kettle, tea and coffee equipment
  ➢ Cool box (for food and cold drinks)
  ➢ Water (for after any track sessions)

CAR RACING TEST AND RACE DAY CHECK LIST

Use this check list each time you are heading to a circuit, whether it is for a track day, test day or a race meeting, and you will never forget your equipment:

➤ Pre-event Admin:
  - ➢ Pay for race entry
  - ➢ Sign on online
  - ➢ Email a photo of race licence to organising club
  - ➢ Scrutineering declaration

➤ Admin:
  - ➢ Tickets (print e-tickets for MSV circuits beforehand)
  - ➢ Paddock pass (if applicable)
  - ➢ MSUK race licence (make sure it is signed)
  - ➢ Upgrade card
  - ➢ Blue Book
  - ➢ A copy of the final instructions (distributed by your organising club)
  - ➢ A printed timetable for the event (applicable to test days and race meetings)

➤ Racing Equipment:
  - ➢ Race suit
  - ➢ Helmet
  - ➢ Balaclava
  - ➢ Gloves
  - ➢ Boots
  - ➢ Fireproof underwear
  - ➢ HANS device or Simpson FHR

➤ Mechanical Equipment
  ➢ Tools
  ➢ Axle stands
  ➢ Jack
  ➢ Cable ties
  ➢ Gaffer tape
  ➢ Blue roll
  ➢ Tyre pressure gauge
  ➢ Fuel and jerry cans
  ➢ Fuel jug with nozzle (to transfer fuel from the jerry can into your race car)
  ➢ Rainex and anti-fog (if you are in a tin top car. This will help to stop your windows and windscreen steaming up and blocking your vision, particularly on a wet day)

➤ Other Equipment
  ➢ Pop up awning
  ➢ Ratchet straps
  ➢ Car cover (for open top cars on uncovered trailers)
  ➢ Electrical cables
  ➢ Kettle, tea and coffee equipment
  ➢ Cool box (for food and cold drinks)
  ➢ Water (for after any track sessions)

ORGANISING CLUBS

➤ 750 Motor Club – www.750mc.co.uk
The 750 Motor Club is described as the 'home of affordable motorsport'.
With over 20 championships and series under the 750MC banner from
single-seaters to road cars and real tin top race cars, the Club offers an
abundance of entry-level motorsport options.

➤ British Automobile Racing Club – www.barc.net
The BARC organises an eclectic mix of championships and series, from
real club level motorsport to the more high-profile British Touring Car
Championship (BTCC).

➤ British Racing and Sports Car Club – www.brscc.co.uk
The BRSCC hosts everything from saloon and production cars to single-
seaters, sports cars and GT and touring machines.

➤ Classic Sports Car Club – www.classicsportscarclub.co.uk
The CSCC is open to cars that fall into the realm of being considered a
classic. With a total of 12 series to choose from, the CSCC is on a slightly
smaller scale to that of other clubs; however, it offers, fun, friendly,
affordable racing.

➤ Historic Sports Car Club – www.hscc.org.uk
The HSCC is aimed at those wishing to compete in historic motor racing.
With a vast selection of championships that run under the HSCC banner,
there are plenty to choose from for historic motorsport fans.

➤ MG Car Club – www.mgcc.co.uk
The MGCC is heavily centred on the MG brand and road going MG cars,
although its motorsport division has always been extremely popular and
continues to thrive season after season.

➤ MotorSport Vision Racing – www.msvracing.com
Another club that boasts a vast collection of championships and series,
from entry level sprint and endurance races through to the more prominent
events, MSVR features some superb racing, and plenty of budget friendly
options to choose from.

➤ Vintage Sports Car Club – www.vscc.co.uk
A club that falls into the more specialist motorsport category, the VSCC
offers some spectacular action, in some very special vintage machinery.

INSTRUCTOR DIRECTORY

Instructors listed below are some of the best instructors in the UK. Although this is a small list, these are all instructors I would be more than happy to recommend. Contact details for each of them can be found with a simple Google search, with most of them having their own website. Some will also have their own YouTube channel, and these are certainly worth a watch. A list of instructors can also be found on the ARDS website.

➤ Luke Kidsley (Grade A)
➤ David Bailey (Grade S)
➤ Ryan Hooker (Grade S)
➤ Scott Gillam (Grade A)
➤ Ben Clucas (Grade A)
➤ Darren Burke (Grade A)
➤ Jon Barnes (Grade A)
➤ Jonny Adam (Grade A)
➤ Phil Bailey (Grade A)
➤ Andrew Bentley (Grade A)
➤ Neil Boardman (Grade A)
➤ Perry Brewer (Grade A)
➤ Michael Broadhurst (Grade A)
➤ Jamie Stanley (Grade A)
➤ Rory Butcher (Grade A)
➤ Hannah Chapman (Grade B)
➤ Kieran Vernon (Grade A)
➤ Max Coates (Grade A)
➤ Matthew Cowley (Grade B)
➤ Andrew Crighton (Grade S)

UK KART CIRCUITS

- Bayford Meadows (Kent)
- Birmingham Grand Prix (West Midlands)
- Blackbushe/Camberley (Surrey)
- Brentwood (Essex)
- Brighton Kart Circuit (East Sussex)
- Boyndie/Grampion (Scotland)
- Buckmore Park (Kent)
- Clay Pigeon (Dorset)
- Crail Kart Circuit (Scotland)
- Daytona Lydd (Kent)
- Daytona Milton Keynes (Northamptonshire)
- Dunkeswell (Devon)
- Ellough Park (Suffolk)
- Forest Edge (Hampshire)
- Fulbeck Kart Circuit (Lincolnshire)
- Glan Y Gors Kart Circuit (North Wales)
- Golspie Kart Circuit (Scotland)
- Kimbolton Kart Circuit (Cambridgeshire)
- Lakeside Kart Circuit (Essex)
- Larkhall/Summerlee Kart Circuit (Scotland)
- Little Rissington Kart Circuit (Gloucestershire)
- Nutts Corner Kart Circuit (Northern Ireland)
- PF International (Lincolnshire)
- Raceland Kart Circuit (Scotland)
- Raceway Kart Centre (Lincolnshire)
- Rowrah Cumbria Kart Circuit (Cumbria)
- Rye House Kart Circuit (Hertfordshire)
- Sandown Park (Surrey)
- Shenington Kart Circuit (Oxfordshire)
- Teesside Kart Circuit (Middlesbrough)
- Three Sisters Kart Circuit (Greater Manchester)
- Warder Law Kart Circuit (Sunderland)
- Whilton Mill (Northamptonshire)
- Wombwell Kart Circuit (South Yorkshire)
- York Pro-Am Kart Circuit (Yorkshire)

UK RACE CIRCUITS

- ➤ Aintree Circuit (Merseyside)
- ➤ Anglesey Circuit (North Wales)
- ➤ Bedford Autodrome (Bedfordshire)
- ➤ Blyton Park (North Lincolnshire)
- ➤ Brands Hatch (Kent)
- ➤ Cadwell Park (Lincolnshire)
- ➤ Castle Combe (Wiltshire)
- ➤ Croft Circuit (North Yorkshire)
- ➤ Donington Park (Leicestershire)
- ➤ Goodwood Circuit (West Sussex)
- ➤ Knockhill Circuit (Scotland)
- ➤ Lydden Hill (Kent)
- ➤ Mallory Park (Leicestershire)
- ➤ Oulton Park (Cheshire)
- ➤ Pembrey Circuit (South Wales)
- ➤ Silverstone Circuit (Northamptonshire)
- ➤ Snetterton (Norfolk)
- ➤ Thruxton (Hampshire)

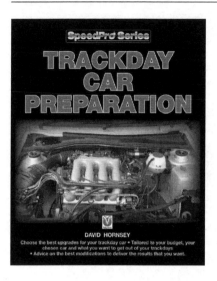

COMPETITION CAR COMPOSITES

A PRACTICAL HANDBOOK

Simon McBeath
Foreword by Brian O'Rourke

REVISED 2nd EDITION

From basic methods to advanced techniques: with chapters covering materials, patterns, moulds, components and technology upgrades applicable to the home workshop, this book will help any reader – whether building, repairing, or developing competition cars or components – exploit composites technology to gain performance advantages.

ISBN: 978-1-845849-05-4
Hardback • 23.3x16.9cm • 208 pages

• email: info@veloce.co.uk • Tel: +44(0)1305 260068

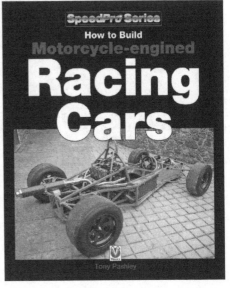

INDEX